Getting Started with Business Communication for Microsoft® Office 2013

Amy Kinser

DIANE L. KOSHAREK

PEARSON

Boston Columbus Indianapolis New York San Francisco Hoboken
Amsterdam Cape Town Dubai London Madrid Milan Munich Paris Montréal Toronto
Delhi Mexico City São Paulo Sydney Hong Kong Seoul Singapore Taipei Tokyo

VP of Career Skills: Andrew Gilfillan
Senior Editor: Samantha McAfee Lewis
Team Lead, Project Management: Laura Burgess
Project Manager: Anne Garcia
Program Manager: Natacha Moore
Development Editor: Barbara Stover
Editorial Assistant: Victoria Lasavath
Director of Product Marketing: Maggie Waples
Product Marketing Manager: Kaylee Carlson
Director of Field Marketing: Leigh Ann Sims
Field Marketing Managers: Brad Forrester & Joanna Sabella
Marketing Coordinator: Susan Osterlitz
Senior Operations Specialist: Diane Peirano
Senior Art Director: Diane Ernsberger
Interior and Cover Design: Diane Ernsberger
Associate Director of Design: Blair Brown
Digital Media Editor: Eric Hakanson
Director of Media Development: Taylor Ragan
Media Project Manager, Production: John Cassar
Full-Service Project Management: GEX Publishing Services
Composition: GEX Publishing Services

Credits and acknowledgments borrowed from other sources and reproduced, with permission, in this textbook appear on the appropriate page within text.

Library of Congress Control Number: 2014946252

10 9 8 7 6 5 4 3 2 1
ISBN-13: 978-0-13-314376-8
ISBN-10: 0-13-314376-7

About the Authors

Amy S. Kinser, Esq., Series Editor

Amy holds a B.A. degree in Chemistry with a Business minor from Indiana University, and a J.D. from the Maurer School of Law, also at Indiana University. After working as an environmental chemist, starting her own technology consulting company, and practicing intellectual property law, she has spent the past 12 years teaching technology at the Kelley School of Business in Bloomington, Indiana—#1 ranked school for undergraduate program performance in the specialty of Information Systems according to 2012 Bloomberg Businessweek. Currently, she serves as the Director of Computer Skills and Senior Lecturer at the Kelley School of Business at Indiana University. She also loves spending time with her two sons, Aidan and J. Matthew, and her husband J. Eric.

I dedicate this series to my Kinser Boyz for their unwavering love, support, and patience; to my family; to my students for inspiring me; to Sam for believing in me; and to the instructors. I hope this series will inspire!
Amy Kinser

Diane L. Kosharek

Diane is a full-time Business Technology faculty member at Madison College in Madison, WI. In addition to her faculty role, she works closely with business and industry specialists, developing and delivering tailored training solutions to employees in areas such as customer service, software applications, and business writing skills. Prior to joining Madison College, she worked as a Technology Training Consultant, providing consultation and production assistance to teaching faculty and staff to incorporate appropriate technology in their courses to enhance learning. Diane holds a Bachelor's Degree in Education from the University of Wisconsin-Madison and a Master's Degree in Educational Computing from Cardinal Stritch University.

To my husband John for his love, patience, and encouragement to follow through with my desire to write; to my sons Alex and Justin for their love and support; to my parents, who pushed me to "do" and told me I could; to a special colleague, Ann, for her help and support; and to the memory of my best friend Betty, who lives on in my heart.
Diane Kosharek

Contents

BUSINESS COMMUNICATION

Acknowledgments

The ***Your Office*** team would like to thank the following reviewers who have invested time and energy to help shape this series from the very beginning, providing us with invaluable feedback through their comments, suggestions, and constructive criticism.

We'd like to especially thank our Focus Group attendees and User Diary Reviewers:

Heather Albinger
Waukesha County Technical College

Melody Alexander
Ball State University

Mazhar Anik
Owens Community College

David Antol
Hartford Community College

Cheryl Brown
Delgado Community College

Janet Campbell
Dixie State College

Kuan Chen
Purdue Calumet

Jennifer Day
Sinclair Community College

Joseph F. Domagala
Duquesne University

Christa Fairman
Arizona Western University

Denise Farley
Sussex County Community College

Drew Foster
Miami University of Ohio

Lorie Goodgine
Tennessee Technology Center in Paris

Jane L. Hammer
Valley City State University

Kay Johnson
Community College of Rhode Island

Susumu Kasai
Salt Lake Community College

Linda Kavanaugh
Robert Morris University

Jennifer Krou
Texas State University, San Marcos

Michelle Mallon
Ohio State University

Sandra McCormack
Monroe Community College

Melissa Nemeth
Indiana University – Purdue University, Indianapolis

Janet Olfert
North Dakota State University

Patsy Ann Parker
Southwestern Oklahoma State University

Cheryl Reindl-Johnson
Sinclair Community College

Jennifer Robinson
Trident Technical College

Tony Rose
Miami University of Ohio

Cindi Smatt
North Georgia College & State University

Jenny Lee Svelund
University of Utah

William VanderClock
Bentley University

Jill Weiss
Florida International University

Lin Zhao
Purdue Calumet

We'd like to thank all of our conscientious reviewers, including those who contributed to our previous editions:

Sven Aelterman
Troy University

Nitin Aggarwal
San Jose State University

Angel Alexander
Piedmont Technical College

Melody Alexander
Ball State University

Karen Allen
Community College of Rhode Island

Maureen Allen
Elon University

Wilma Andrews
Virginia Commonwealth University

Mazhar Anik
Owens Community College

David Antol
Harford Community College

Kirk Atkinson
Western Kentucky University

Barbara Baker
Indiana Wesleyan University

Kristi Berg
Minot State University

Kavuri Bharath
Old Dominion University

Ann Blackman
Parkland College

Jeanann Boyce
Montgomery College

Lynn Brooks
Tyler Junior College

Cheryl Brown
Delgado Community College, West Bank Campus

Bonnie Buchanan
Central Ohio Technical College

Peggy Burrus
Red Rocks Community College

Richard Cacace
Pensacola State College

Margo Chaney
Carroll Community College

Shanan Chappell
College of the Albemarle, North Carolina

Kuan Chen
Purdue Calumet

David Childress
Ashland Community and Technical College

Keh-Wen Chuang
Purdue University, North Central

Suzanne Clayton
Drake University

Amy Clubb
Portland Community College

Bruce Collins
Davenport University

Margaret Cooksey
Tallahassee Community College

Charmayne Cullom
University of Northern Colorado

Christy Culver
Marion Technical College

Juliana Cypert
Tarrant County College

Harold Davis
Southeastern Louisiana University

Jeff Davis
Jamestown Community College

Jennifer Day
Sinclair Community College

Anna Degtyareva
Mt. San Antonio College

Beth Deinert
Southeast Community College

Kathleen DeNisco
Erie Community College

Donald Dershem
Mountain View College

Bambi Edwards
Craven Community College

Elaine Emanuel
Mt. San Antonio College

Diane Endres
Ancilla College

Nancy Evans
Indiana University – Purdue University, Indianapolis

Christa Fairman
Arizona Western College

Marni Ferner
University of North Carolina, Wilmington

Paula Fisher
Central New Mexico Community College

Linda Fried
University of Colorado, Denver

Diana Friedman
Riverside Community College

Susan Fry
Boise State University

Virginia Fullwood
Texas A&M University, Commerce

Janos Fustos
Metropolitan State College of Denver

John Fyfe
University of Illinois at Chicago

Saiid Ganjalizadeh
The Catholic University of America

Randolph Garvin
Tyler Junior College

Diane Glowacki
Tarrant County College

Jerome Gonnella
Northern Kentucky University

Connie Grimes
Morehead State University

Debbie Gross
Ohio State University

Babita Gupta
California State University, Monterey Bay

Lewis Hall
Riverside City College

Jane Hammer
Valley City State University

Marie Hartlein
Montgomery County Community College

Darren Hayes
Pace University

Paul Hayes
Eastern New Mexico University

Mary Hedberg
Johnson County Community College

Lynda Henrie
LDS Business College

Deedee Herrera
Dodge City Community College

Marilyn Hibbert
Salt Lake Community College

Jan Hime
University of Nebraska, Lincoln

Cheryl Hinds
Norfolk State University

Mary Kay Hinkson
Fox Valley Technical College

Margaret Hohly
Cerritos College

Brian Holbert
Spring Hill College

Susan Holland
Southeast Community College

Anita Hollander
University of Tennessee, Knoxville

Emily Holliday
Campbell University

Stacy Hollins
St. Louis Community College, Florissant Valley

Mike Horn
State University of New York, Geneseo

Christie Hovey
Lincoln Land Community College

Margaret Hvatum
St. Louis Community College, Meramec

Jean Insinga
Middlesex Community College

Jon (Sean) Jasperson
Texas A&M University

Glen Jenewein
Kaplan University

Gina Jerry
Santa Monica College

Dana Johnson
North Dakota State University

Mary Johnson
Mt. San Antonio College

Linda Johnsonius
Murray State University

Carla Jones
Middle Tennessee State University

Susan Jones
Utah State University

Nenad Jukic
Loyola University, Chicago

Sali Kaceli
Philadelphia Biblical University

Sue Kanda
Baker College of Auburn Hills

Robert Kansa
Macomb Community College

Susumu Kasai
Salt Lake Community College

Linda Kavanaugh
Robert Morris University

Debby Keen
University of Kentucky

Mike Kelly
Community College of Rhode Island

Melody Kiang
California State University, Long Beach

Lori Kielty
College of Central Florida

Richard Kirk
Pensacola State College

Dawn Konicek
Blackhawk Tech

John Kucharczuk
Centennial College

David Largent
Ball State University

Frank Lee
Fairmont State University

Luis Leon
The University of Tennessee at Chattanooga

Freda Leonard
Delgado Community College

Julie Lewis
Baker College, Allen Park

Suhong Li
Bryant University

Renee Lightner
Florida State College

John Lombardi
South University

Rhonda Lucas
Spring Hill College

Adriana Lumpkin
Midland College

Lynne Lyon
Durham College

Nicole Lytle
California State University,
San Bernardino

Donna Madsen
Kirkwood Community College

Susan Maggio
Community College of
Baltimore County

Kim Manning
Tallahassee Community College

Paul Martin
Harrisburg Area Community College

Cheryl Martucci
Diablo Valley College

Sebena Masline
Florida State College of Jacksonville

Sherry Massoni
Harford Community College

Lee McClain
Western Washington University

Sandra McCormack
Monroe Community College

Sue McCrory
Missouri State University

Barbara Miller
University of Notre Dame

Michael O. Moorman
Saint Leo University

Kathleen Morris
University of Alabama

Alysse Morton
Westminster College

Elobaid Muna
University of Maryland Eastern Shore

Jackie Myers
Sinclair Community College

Russell Myers
El Paso Community College

Bernie Negrete
Cerritos College

Melissa Nemeth
Indiana University – Purdue University,
Indianapolis

Jennifer Nightingale
Duquesne University

Kathie O'Brien
North Idaho College

Michael Ogawa
University of Hawaii

Rene Pack
Arizona Western College

Patsy Parker
Southwest Oklahoma State University

Laurie Patterson
University of North Carolina, Wilmington

Alicia Pearlman
Baker College

Diane Perreault
Sierra College and California State University,
Sacramento

Theresa Phinney
Texas A&M University

Vickie Pickett
Midland College

Marcia Polanis
Forsyth Technical Community College

Rose Pollard
Southeast Community College

Stephen Pomeroy
Norwich University

Leonard Presby
William Paterson University

Donna Reavis
Delta Career Education

Eris Reddoch
Pensacola State College

James Reddoch
Pensacola State College

Michael Redmond
La Salle University

Terri Rentfro
John A. Logan College

Vicki Robertson
Southwest Tennessee Community College

Dianne Ross
University of Louisiana at Lafayette

Ann Rowlette
Liberty University

Amy Rutledge
Oakland University

Candace Ryder
Colorado State University

Joann Segovia
Winona State University

Eileen Shifflett
James Madison University

Sandeep Shiva
Old Dominion University

Robert Sindt
Johnson County Community College

Cindi Smatt
Texas A&M University

Edward Souza
Hawaii Pacific University

Nora Spencer
Fullerton College

Alicia Stonesifer
La Salle University

Cheryl Sypniewski
Macomb Community College

Arta Szathmary
Bucks County Community College

Nasser Tadayon
Southern Utah University

Asela Thomason
California State University Long Beach

Nicole Thompson
Carteret Community College

Terri Tiedema
Southeast Community College, Nebraska

Lewis Todd
Belhaven University

Barb Tollinger
Sinclair Community College

Allen Truell
Ball State University

Erhan Uskup
Houston Community College

Lucia Vanderpool
Baptist College of Health Sciences

Michelle Vlaich-Lee
Greenville Technical College

Barry Walker
Monroe Community College

Rosalyn Warren
Enterprise State Community College

Sonia Washington
Prince George's Community College

Eric Weinstein
Suffolk County Community College

Jill Weiss
Florida International University

Lorna Wells
Salt Lake Community College

Rosalie Westerberg
Clover Park Technical College

Clemetee Whaley
Southwest Tennessee Community College

Kenneth Whitten
Florida State College of Jacksonville

MaryLou Wilson
Piedmont Technical College

John Windsor
University of North Texas

Kathy Winters
University of Tennessee, Chattanooga

Nancy Woolridge
Fullerton College

Jensen Zhao
Ball State University

Martha Zimmer
University of Evansville

Molly Zimmer
University of Evansville

Mary Anne Zlotow
College of DuPage

Matthew Zullo
Wake Technical Community College

Additionally, we'd like to thank our MyITLab team for their review and collaboration with our text authors:

LeeAnn Bates

Jennifer Hurley

Ralph Moore

Jerri Williams

Jaimie Noy
Media Producer

Preface

The ***Your Office*** series focuses first and foremost on preparing students to use both technical and soft skills in the real world. Our goal is to provide this to both instructors and students through a modern approach to teaching and learning Microsoft Office applications, an approach that weaves in the technical content using a realistic business scenario and focuses on using Office as a decision-making tool.

The process of developing this unique series for you, the modern student or instructor, requires innovative ideas regarding the pedagogy and organization of the text. You learn best when doing—so you will be active from Page 1. Your learning goes to the next level when you are challenged to do more with less—your hand will be held at first but, progressively, the case exercises require more from you. Because you care about how things work in the real world—in your classes, your future jobs, your personal life—Real World Advice, Videos, and Success Stories are woven throughout the text. These innovative features will help you progress from a basic understanding of Office to mastery of each application, empowering you to perform with confidence in Windows 8, Word, Excel, Access, and PowerPoint, including on mobile devices.

No matter what career you may choose to pursue in life, this series will give you the foundation to succeed. ***Your Office*** uses cases that will enable you to be immersed in a realistic business as you learn Office in the context of a running business scenario—the Painted Paradise Resort & Spa. You will immediately delve into the many interesting, smaller businesses in this resort (golf course, spa, restaurants, hotel, etc.) to learn how a larger organization actually uses Office. You will learn how to make Office work for you now, as a student, and in your future career.

Today, the experience of working with Office is not isolated to working in a job in a cubicle. Your physical office is wherever you are with a laptop or a mobile device. Office has changed. It's modern. It's mobile. It's personal. And when you learn these valuable skills and master Office, you are able to make Office your own. The title of this series is a promise to you, the student: Our goal is to make Microsoft Office ***Your Office***.

Key Features

- **Starting and Ending Files:** These appear before every case in the text. Starting Files identify exactly which Student Data Files are needed to complete each case. Ending Files are provided to show students the naming conventions they should use when saving their files. Each file icon is color coded by application.
- **Workshop Objectives List:** The learning objectives to be achieved as students work through the workshop. Page numbers are included for easy reference. These are revisited in the Concept Check at the end of the workshop.
- **Real World Success:** A boxed feature in the workshop opener that shares an anecdote from a real former student, describing how knowledge of Office has helped him or her to get ahead or be successful in his or her life.
- **Active Text Box:** Represents the active portion of the workshop and is easily distinguishable from explanatory text by the blue shaded background. Active Text helps students quickly identify what steps they need to follow to complete the workshop Prepare Case.
- **Quick Reference Box:** A boxed feature in the workshop, summarizing generic or alternative instructions on how to accomplish a task. This feature enables students to quickly find important skills.
- **Real World Advice Box:** A boxed feature in the workshop, offering advice and best practices for general use of important Office skills. The goal is to advise students as a manager might in a future job.
- **Side Note:** A brief tip or piece of information aligned visually with a step in the workshop, quickly providing key information to students completing that particular step.
- **Consider This:** In-text critical thinking questions and topics for discussion, set apart as a boxed feature, allowing students to step back from the project and think about the application of what they are learning and how these concepts might be used in the future.
- **Concept Check:** Review questions appearing at the end of the workshop, which require students to demonstrate their understanding of the objectives in that workshop.
- **Visual Summary:** A visual review of the objectives learned in the workshop using images from the completed solution file, mapped to the workshop objectives using callouts and page references so students can easily find the section of text to refer to for a refresher.
- **Business Application Icons:** Appear with every case in the text and clearly identify which business application students are being exposed to, for example, Finance, Marketing, Operations, etc.

Business Application Icons

Customer Service

Finance & Accounting

General Business

Human Resources

Information Technology

Production & Operations

Sales & Marketing

Research & Development

Instructor Resources

The Instructor's Resource Center, available at www.pearsonhighered.com, includes the following:

- Prepared Exams with solution files for additional assessment.
- Annotated Solution Files with Scorecards to assist with grading the Prepare, Practice, Problem Solve, and Perform Cases.
- Data and Solution Files.
- Rubrics for Perform Cases in Microsoft Word format to enable instructors to easily grade open-ended assignments with no definite solution.
- PowerPoint Presentations with notes for each chapter.
- Instructor's Manual that provides detailed blueprints to achieve workshop learning objectives and outcomes and best use the unique structure of the modules.
- Complete Test Bank, also available in TestGen format.
- Syllabus templates.
- Additional Practice, Problem Solve, and Perform Cases to provide you with variety and choice in exercises both on the workshop and module levels.
- Scripted Lectures to provide instructors with a lecture outline that mirrors the Workshop Prepare Case.
- Flexible, robust, and customizable content is available for all major online course platforms that include everything instructors need in one place. Please contact your sales representative for information on accessing course cartridges for WebCT or Blackboard.

Student Resources

- Companion Website
- Student Data Files

Pearson's Companion Website

www.pearsonhighered.com/youroffice offers expanded IT resources and downloadable supplements. Students can find the following self-study tools for each workshop:

- Online Workshop Review
- Workshop Objectives
- Glossary
- Student Data Files

Dear Students,

If you want an edge over the competition, make it personal. Whether you love sports, travel, the stock market, or ballet, your passion is personal to you. Capitalizing on your passion leads to success. You live in a global marketplace, and your competition is global. The honors students in China exceed the total number of students in North America. Skills can help set you apart, but passion will make you stand above. ***Your Office*** is the tool to harness your passion's true potential.

In prior generations, personalization in a professional setting was discouraged. You had a "work" life and a "home" life. As the Series Editor, I write to you about the vision for ***Your Office*** from my laptop, on my couch, in the middle of the night when inspiration strikes me. My classroom and living room are my office. Life has changed from generations before us.

So, let's get personal. My degrees are not in technology, but chemistry and law. I helped put myself through school by working full time in various jobs, including a successful technology consulting business that continues today. My generation did not grow up with computers, but I did. My father was a network administrator for the military. So, I was learning to program in Basic before anyone had played Nintendo's Duck Hunt or Tetris. Technology has always been one of my passions from a young age. In fact, I now tell my husband: don't buy me jewelry for my birthday, buy me the latest gadget on the market!

In my first law position, I was known as the Office guru to the extent that no one gave me a law assignment for the first two months. Once I submitted the assignment, my supervisor remarked, "Wow, you don't just know how to leverage technology, but you really know the law too." I can tell you novel-sized stories from countless prior students in countless industries who gained an edge from using Office as a tool. Bringing technology to your passion makes you well-rounded and a cut above the rest, no matter the industry or position.

I am most passionate about teaching, in particular teaching technology. I come from many generations of teachers, including my mother who is a kindergarten teacher. For over 12 years, I have found my dream job passing on my passion for teaching, technology, law, science, music, and life in general at the Kelley School of Business at Indiana University. I have tried to pass on the key to engaging passion to my students. I have helped them see what differentiates them from all the other bright students vying for the same jobs.

Microsoft Office is a tool. All of your competition will have learned Microsoft Office to some degree or another. Some will have learned it to an advanced level. Knowing Microsoft Office is important, but it is also fundamental. Without it, you will not be considered for a position.

Today, you step into your first of many future roles bringing Microsoft Office to your dream job working for Painted Paradise Resort & Spa. You will delve into the business side of the resort and learn how to use ***Your Office*** to maximum benefit.

Don't let the context of a business fool you. If you don't think of yourself as a business person, you have no need to worry. Whether you realize it or not, everything is business. If you want to be a nurse, you are entering the health care industry. If you want to be a football player in the NFL, you are entering the business of sports as entertainment. In fact, if you want to be a stay-at-home parent, you are entering the business of a family household where ***Your Office*** still gives you an advantage. For example, you will be able to prepare a budget in Excel and analyze what you need to do to afford a trip to Disney World!

At Painted Paradise Resort & Spa, you will learn how to make Office yours through four learning levels designed to maximize your understanding. You will Prepare, Practice, and Problem Solve your tasks. Then, you will astound when you Perform your new talents. You will be challenged through Consider This questions and gain insight through Real World Advice.

There is something more. You want success in what you are passionate about in your life. It is personal for you. In this position at Painted Paradise Resort & Spa, you will gain your personal competitive advantage that will stay with you for the rest of your life—***Your Office***.

Sincerely,

Amy Kinser

Series Editor

Painted Paradise

RESORT & SPA

Welcome to the Team!

Welcome to your new office at Painted Paradise Resort & Spa, where we specialize in painting perfect getaways. As the Chief Technology Officer, I am excited to have staff dedicated to the Microsoft Office integration between all the areas of the resort. Our team is passionate about our paradise, and I hope you find this to be your dream position here!

Painted Paradise is a resort and spa in New Mexico catering to business people, romantics, families, and anyone who just needs to get away. Inside our resort are many distinct areas. Many of these areas operate as businesses in their own right but must integrate with the other areas of the resort. The main areas of the resort are as follows.

- The **Hotel** is overseen by our Chief Executive Officer, William Mattingly, and is at the core of our business. The hotel offers a variety of accommodations, ranging from individual rooms to a grand villa suite. Further, the hotel offers packages including spa, golf, and special events.

  Room rates vary according to size, season, demand, and discount. The hotel has discounts for typical groups, such as AARP. The hotel also has a loyalty program where guests can earn free nights based on frequency of visits. Guests may charge anything from the resort to the room.

- **Red Bluff Golf Course** is a private world-class golf course and pro shop. The golf course has services such as golf lessons from the famous golf pro John Schilling and playing packages. Also, the golf course attracts local residents. This requires variety in pricing schemes to accommodate both local and hotel guests. The pro shop sells many retail items online.

  The golf course can also be reserved for special events and tournaments. These special events can be in conjunction with a wedding, conference, meetings, or other event covered by the event planning and catering area of the resort.

- **Turquoise Oasis Spa** is a full-service spa. Spa services include haircuts, pedicures, massages, facials, body wraps, waxing, and various other spa services—typical to exotic. Further, the spa offers private consultation, weight training (in the fitness center), a water bar, meditation areas, and steam rooms. Spa services are offered both in the spa and in the resort guest's room.

  Turquoise Oasis Spa uses top-of-the-line products and some house-brand products. The retail side offers products ranging from candles to age-defying home treatments. These products can also be purchased online. Many of the hotel guests who fall in love with the house-brand soaps, lotions, candles, and other items appreciate being able to buy more at any time.

  The spa offers a multitude of packages including special hotel room packages that include spa treatments. Local residents also use the spa. So, the spa guests are not limited to hotel guests. Thus, the packages also include pricing attractive to the local community.

Painted Paradise

Red Bluff Golf Course & Pro Shop

- **Painted Treasures Gift Shop** has an array of items available for purchase, from toiletries to clothes to presents for loved ones back home including a healthy section of kids' toys for traveling business people. The gift shop sells a small sampling from the spa, golf course pro shop, and local New Mexico culture. The gift shop also has a small section of snacks and drinks. The gift shop has numerous part-time employees including students from the local college.
- **The Event Planning & Catering** area is central to attracting customers to the resort. From weddings to conferences, the resort is a popular destination. The resort has a substantial number of staff dedicated to planning, coordinating, setting up, catering, and maintaining these events. The resort has several facilities that can accommodate large groups. Packages and prices vary by size, room, and other services such as catering. Further, the Event Planning & Catering team works closely with local vendors for floral decorations, photography, and other event or wedding typical needs. However, all catering must go through the resort (no outside catering permitted). Lastly, the resort stocks several choices of decorations, table arrangements, and centerpieces. These range from professional, simple, themed, and luxurious.
- **Indigo5** and the **Silver Moon Lounge**, a world-class restaurant and lounge that is overseen by the well-known Chef Robin Sanchez. The cuisine is balanced and modern. From steaks to pasta to local southwestern meals, Indigo5 attracts local patrons in addition to resort guests. While the catering function is separate from the restaurant—though menu items may be shared—the restaurant does support all room service for the resort. The resort also has smaller food venues onsite such as the Terra Cotta Brew coffee shop in the lobby.

Currently, these areas are using Office to various degrees. In some areas, paper and pencil are still used for most business functions. Others have been lucky enough to have some technology savvy team members start Microsoft Office Solutions.

Using your skills, I am confident that you can help us integrate and use Microsoft Office on a whole new level! I hope you are excited to call Painted Paradise Resort & Spa ***Your Office***.

Looking forward to working with you more closely!

Aidan Matthews

Aidan Matthews
Chief Technology Officer

Business Communication
Module 1

WORKSHOP 1 | DEVELOPING FOUNDATIONS OF EFFECTIVE BUSINESS COMMUNICATION

OBJECTIVES

1. Understand the communication process p. 4
2. Understand the business writing process p. 9
3. Prepare written messages p. 13
4. Apply strategies for writing messages p. 21
5. Understand how digital communication is transforming the workplace p. 23
6. Use effective oral communication skills in the workplace p. 28

Prepare Case

Conference Center Internship: Publications

© Stephen Coburn/Fotolia

Congratulations! You have been selected to join the Painted Paradise Golf Resort and Spa Conference Center team as a virtual assistant. You will have a mentor who will accompany you throughout the first months, answer questions, and act as a guide. Under the supervision of Lesa Martin, you will be responsible for writing, editing, and designing various internal and external publications; reviewing and evaluating documents to ensure clarity and consistency; preparing and updating print and electronic communications, including digital presentations, flyers, fact sheets, news releases, and other related reports; and planning the Resort's annual employee appreciation banquet.

REAL WORLD SUCCESS

"I learned in my first position out of college how valuable excellent communication skills were. Working on and improving my communication style advanced my career faster than having great technology skills."

- Lauren, alumnus and Account Manager Coordinator

Student data files needed for this workshop:

- bc01ws01CulturalDifferences.pptx
- bc01ws01ActiveVoice.docx
- bc01ws01EventPlanningLogo.jpg
- bc01ws01FormattingReport.docx
- bc01ws01YouAttitude.docx
- bc01ws01EmailSubjectLines.docx
- bc01ws01Resort.pptx

You will save your files as:

- bc01ws01CulturalDifferences_LastFirst.pptx
- bc01ws01ActiveVoice_LastFirst.docx
- bc01ws01Letterhead_LastFirst.docx
- bc01ws01LetterheadTemplate_LastFirst.dotx
- bc01ws01MemoTemplate_LastFirst.dotx
- bc01ws01FormattingReport_LastFirst.docx
- bc01ws01YouAttitude_LastFirst.docx
- bc01ws01EmailSubjectLines_LastFirst.docx
- bc01ws01Resort_LastFirst.pptx

Communicating Effectively

Every business, large and small, relies on communication. Developing excellent communication skills will be a key factor in your success at work and in your personal life. In order to improve your communication skills, you will need to understand how the communication process works.

Understand the Communication Process

The explosion of digital technology and globalization requires businesses to look for talented individuals who can communicate effectively. Good writing, speaking, and listening skills will positively impact your success at work.

Studies show that the ability to communicate effectively in the workplace is one of the top-ranked skills employers are looking for in potential new hires. According to the National Association of Colleges and Employers Job Outlook 2013 survey, employers are looking at job applicants who have strong written and oral communication skills as well as leadership and problem-solving skills. The ability to work in teams is also a top-rated skill.

REAL WORLD ADVICE | **The Importance of Written and Oral Communication**

Considered soft skills, excellent written and oral communications are often the factors that set individuals apart from others in a company. Their importance cannot be overstated. These skills can identify you as one of the most valued employees in the workplace. Your performance will be judged on your ability to communicate effectively. Take the time to hone these skills.

Exploring the Communication Process

Even though technology is changing the way we communicate at a faster rate than ever before, the basic principles for effective communication remain the same. You must not only disseminate information among individuals correctly, but you must also ensure that the information disseminated is understood. Understanding how the communication process works will help you improve your communication skills and help to ensure that your intended message is understood.

Communication can be defined as the exchange of information from one individual or group to another. All communication requires a sender, a message, and a recipient. Communication cannot be a one-way exchange. For effective communication to take place, there must be a two-way exchange in which shared meaning and understanding takes place between the sender and the receiver over a channel. A **channel** is the medium in which the message is sent to its intended audience.

Figure 1 is a simplistic representation of a complex process for the exchange of information. The six basic components of this process are defined below:

- Sender—The sender generates an idea.
- Message—The sender puts the idea into a message (encodes).
- Channel—The message is sent over a channel that is determined by the sender (telephone, fax, memo, e-mail, report, letter, or another channel).
- Noise—Any factor that interferes with the message between the sender and the recipient. It can be physical, psychological, or semantic.
- Receiver—The receiver of the message interprets the message for meaning (decodes).
- Feedback—The receiver provides feedback to the sender. Feedback is the key to whether or not the intended message is understood.

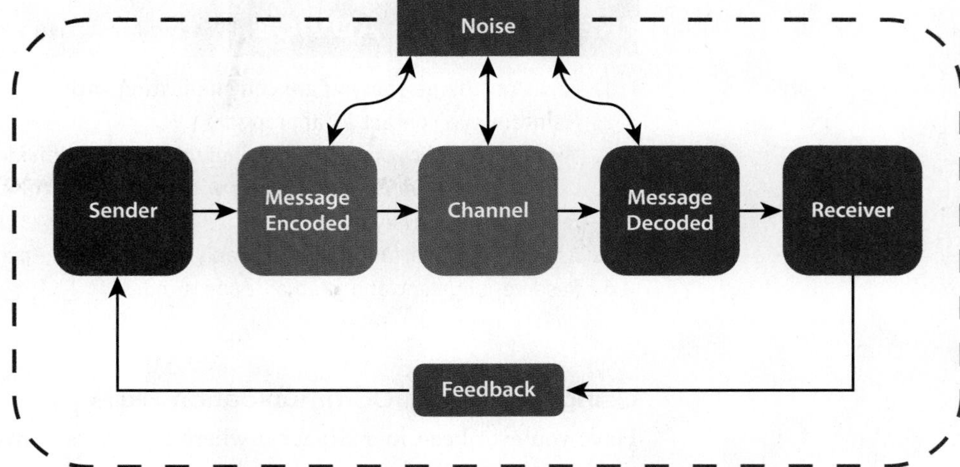

Figure 1 The communication process

Practicing Listening Skills

Listening is something we do all the time, so it should be easy, right? Actually the answer to that question is no. Listening is not easy and studies confirm that most of us are poor listeners. Various studies also confirm that we spend about 80% of our time in some mode of communication. Of that time, 9% is spent writing, 16% reading, 30% speaking, and 45% listening.

If we do not listen effectively, messages are misunderstood and communication breaks down. Since we spend more time listening than we spend doing any other form of communication, it is important that you understand the difference between hearing and listening. **Hearing** is a physical ability that requires no additional intellectual effort. As long as you are physically equipped to receive sounds, you can hear. **Listening** is an active process that requires both hearing and thinking.

In order to become a better listener, you need to practice active listening. **Active listening** involves listening with more than just your ears; it involves your entire body and mind as shown in Figure 2. It takes a lot of effort, practice, and concentration to be an active listener. Being an active listener will make you more productive at work, help you build relationships with others, avoid misunderstandings, as well as help you to work better in a team-based environment.

Figure 2 Listening is essential to good communication

REAL WORLD ADVICE	Steps for Active Listening

1. Focus on the person you are communicating with.
2. Maintain eye contact as appropriate.
3. Minimize distractions. Give the individual your undivided attention.
4. Let the individual finish speaking without interruptions. Do not try to formulate your response while they are speaking.
5. Ask questions for understanding and summarize the main points.
6. Reserve judgment and keep an open mind.

Using Nonverbal Communication Skills

Have you ever been in a situation where a person's nonverbal cues are contradicting the verbal message? What your nonverbal cues are saying may tell the story more than your spoken words. People tend to believe the nonverbal messages more than the verbal messages. Effective communicators are aware of their nonverbal cues and make sure they are not getting in the way of the intended message.

Nonverbal communication includes all unwritten and unspoken messages. Individuals interpret our nonverbal cues in different ways based upon their personal experiences and perceptions. Different cultures may interpret nonverbal cues differently, so being aware of these differences is vital to being a good communicator. Table 1 outlines some of the types of nonverbal communication cues that are important to understand.

Nonverbal Communication	
Posture	The way you position your body. Slouching, leaning, and arm crossing are examples. Posture is often used to evaluate an individual's degree of attention or involvement.
Gestures	Gestures include movement of the hands, arms, head, or other parts of the body. Waving and pointing are examples of gestures. Gestures can convey different meanings in other cultures. For instance, the thumbs-up or a peace sign have different meanings outside of the United States.
Eye Contact	Eyes communicate more than any other part of the body. Excessive blinking, staring, and rolling of the eyes are perceived as negative.
Facial Expressions	Expressions on your face reveal much about what you are really communicating. Your face signals such things as happiness, sadness, boredom, or relaxation.
Voice	The way in which a message is spoken is often as important as what is said. The volume, tone, and rate of speech reveal much about the actual meaning. Your tone of voice can reveal sarcasm, frustration or agreement. We often say that you can "hear" a smile on the phone.

Table 1 Nonverbal communication cues

Communicating Across Cultures

Modern technology and globalization have changed the marketplace for where we do business. Individuals from various cultures are increasingly doing business with each other. Our domestic workplace is also more diverse than before as shown in Figure 3. Because of this shift, it is important that individuals learn to communicate across cultures.

Figure 3 The workplace is more diverse than before

Language differences can pose a huge barrier when attempting to communicate with an individual from another culture. Most American schools do not require students to learn a second language, and thus most Americans do not speak a second language. When communicating with individuals from another culture, we often expect them to speak our language.Think about how many times you have misunderstood someone who speaks your language, and then imagine how hard it may be for someone from a different culture.

Stereotyping people from other cultures is another communication barrier we often see in the workplace. When we **stereotype**, we make assumptions that are not based on truth, but rather what we have heard or believe to be true. For example, Europeans believe Americans are rude and pushy. Not all Americans are rude and pushy, but think how assumptions like this can get in the way of communicating.

Being ignorant of another person's culture can seriously impede your ability to communicate. Taking the time to educate yourself about another individual's culture will allow you to be more open-minded and expand opportunities for building a working relationship.

REAL WORLD ADVICE | **Tips for Better Communication Across Cultures**

- Keep the message simple.
- Attempt to learn the basics about the individual's culture.
- Listen actively.
- Understand how nonverbal cues are different.

It is also important to recognize that there are many differences across cultures in the interpretation of nonverbal cues. Other cultures also attribute different degrees of importance to verbal and nonverbal cues. For example, Japan places a great deal of emphasis on nonverbal cues. Did you know that the simple gesture that Americans use to indicate everything is okay is a very offensive gesture in many parts of the world?

As you become more culturally aware, you will need to understand and learn about cultural differences in relation to personal space, touch, eye contact, time, gestures, and even colors and styles of clothing. All of these can impede an individual's ability to build a positive rapport with coworkers, clients, or customers from a different culture and break down the channels of communication.

Understanding Barriers to Effective Communication

Even the best communicator occasionally has a communication breakdown. Both the sender and the receiver bring their own unique experiences to the communication process. Sometimes these experiences may interfere with the intended message being transmitted. Anything that interferes with the sender's intended message reaching the receiver accurately is considered a **barrier**.

Communication barriers can affect how you interact in the workplace. When the sender initiates a message, the receiver decodes the message and provides feedback. Sometimes there is no feedback, incorrect feedback, or negative feedback. When a receiver is unable to decode a message correctly, there is a breakdown in communication. A breakdown in communication, which can be caused by internal and external factors, takes many forms.

When there is a breakdown in the communication flow, there is at least one communication barrier somewhere in the communication process that can appear anywhere in the communication process. Figure 4 shows some of the common communication barriers.

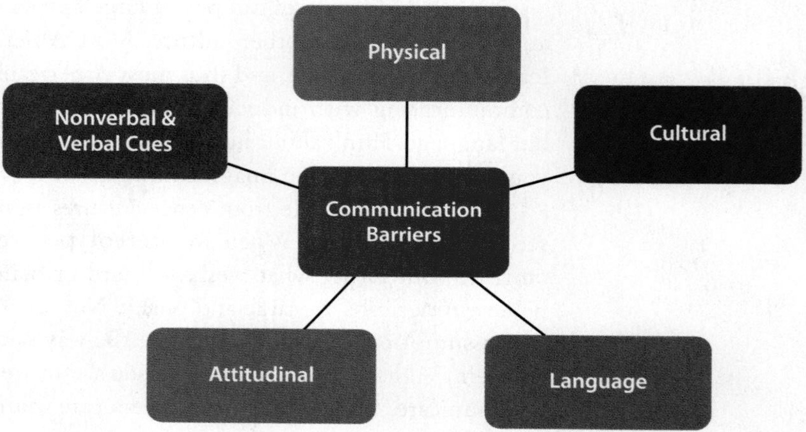

Figure 4 Communication barriers

Common communication barriers are as follows:

- Physical barriers include such things as too much noise, poor lighting, improper heating, and an overall uncomfortable work environment. If the sender and receiver are remotely located, inadequate communication tools can be a physical barrier.
- Cultural barriers refer to miscommunications because of an individual's religion, race, or heritage.
- Attitudinal barriers are created as a result of emotions, state of mind, or personal feelings about an individual or subject.
- Language barriers are created because of a difference in language or lack of appropriate vocabulary.
- Nonverbal messages or verbal cues can replace, strengthen, or contradict verbal messages. They include behaviors such as facial expressions, eyes, touching, tone of voice, voice inflection, accent, etc.

CONSIDER THIS | Communication Breakdowns

What happens when communication breaks down in the workplace? What is the impact on the business? Businesses lose time, money, and opportunities; and it can even impact their reputation. Can you think of any other impacts a business may suffer due to a breakdown in communication?

In this exercise, you will create a PowerPoint presentation that identifies some of the cultural differences between Americans and the Japanese in regard to personal space, touch, eye contact, and gestures.

BC01.00 To Understand Cultural Differences in Nonverbal Communication

a. From the Start screen or desktop, point to **the bottom-right** corner of the screen. The Charms will be displayed on the right side of the screen. Click the **Search** charm. Click inside the **search** box at the top of the page. Type PowerPoint.

b. Click **PowerPoint 2013** in the search results. The PowerPoint Start screen displays.

c. Click **Open Other Presentations**. Double-click **Computer**, and then navigate to where your student data files are located, click **bc01ws01CulturalDifferences**, and then click **Open**.

d. Click the **FILE** tab, and save the file in the location where you are saving your files with the name bc01ws01CulturalDifferences_LastFirst, using your last name and first name.

e. On Slide 1, replace **Presenter Name** with your name.

f. Click on **Slide 2**, and using the Internet to do research, type at least four bullets describing the differences between Americans and Japanese in regards to personal space and touching.

g. Click on **Slide 3**, and using the Internet to do research, type at least three bullet points describing the differences in eye contact for both cultures.

h. Click on **Slide 4**, and using the Internet to do research, type at least three gestures that are significantly different and could cause a communication breakdown between these two cultures.

i. Click on **Slide 5**. Using the APA format, type the sources used for this presentation. Save the presentation and close PowerPoint.

Understand the Business Writing Process

Writing is a process that involves a series of sequential steps. Inexperienced writers often try to skip these steps, and thus they struggle in their effort to produce a well-written document. In reality, to produce a professional business document, you need to plan, write, and revise multiple drafts before you have a well-written finished product. A rule of thumb for inexperienced writers is to spend at least a third of your time in each stage of the writing process outlined in Figure 5.

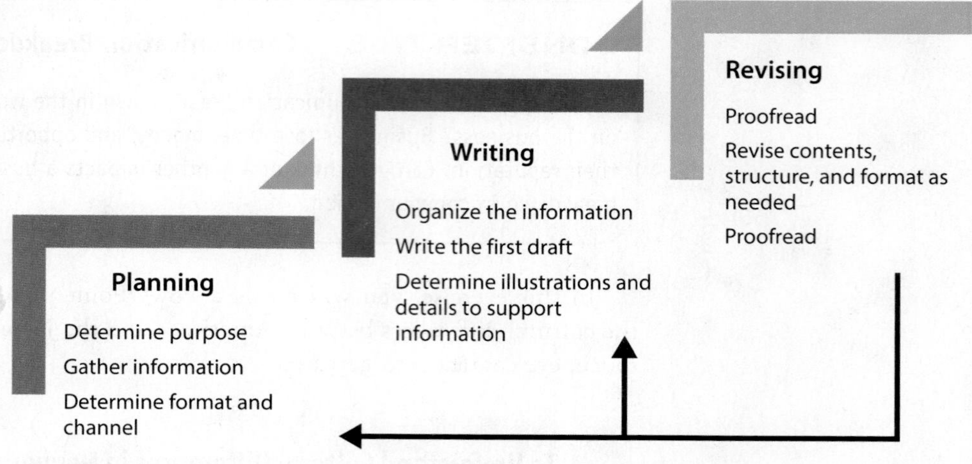

Figure 5 Writing process

Planning for Writing

Planning is the first step in the writing process. This part of the writing process can be broken down into three stages: determining the purpose of the writing, gathering and collecting information, and determining the best method of presenting the information.

During the first stage, you determine the purpose of the message. Why are you writing to the audience? Business messages generally are used to inform or persuade the audience. The purpose helps to define what the intended message needs to accomplish.

Next, you begin to gather information. In this stage you need to define the needs of the audience. Once you know their needs, you can then begin to gather information that is beneficial to them. Gathering information can mean doing formal or informal research. If your message is simple, it may require little research as you may already have all of the needed information. For more complex messages, you may have to spend considerable time researching and analyzing information before you can begin the writing process.

The final stage of the planning step is to determine the channel. How are you planning to deliver your message? Are you planning to send it electronically, through interoffice mail, or through postal mail?

CONSIDER THIS | **What is the best channel? What are some other factors?**

Determining the best channel can depend on several factors:

- What is the speed at which the message needs to be communicated and feedback received?
- Does it contain sensitive, emotional, or confidential information?
- Is a permanent record needed?
- How many people need to receive this information?
- What is the most efficient way to reach all of them?

Writing the Message

During this step you begin to write your first draft. You know the information you want to include, have gathered the information needed, know the purpose, and the intended audience. You are now ready to start composing.

First drafts are often written quickly, allowing the writer to get the main ideas down on paper. Do not worry about perfection at this point. Allow yourself to write a less-than-perfect first draft. Revisions occur at the last stage of the writing process.

Approaching your writing from the audience's viewpoint will help you to recognize what is more likely to be understood or misunderstood. Use simple, direct language in your writing. The more concrete and specific your communication is, the more focused it will be, reducing the chances for any misunderstanding. Most often, you will want to use concrete words over abstract words in your writing.

Abstract words are ideas or concepts. **Concrete words** are explicit words that refer to definite persons, places, or things. Abstract words are useful and necessary in their proper places, but their meanings can be ambiguous. Write using concrete and specific words so your readers can picture what you are saying.

QUICK REFERENCE | **Abstract Versus Concrete Words**

Abstract words—love, happiness, trust, sincerity
Concrete words—chair, box, table, book

Concrete words provide powerful images through the five senses—touch, taste, sight, smell, and hearing. Using concrete and specific words helps the receiver to understand what you mean. Specific words make your writing more accurate. They help to put a clear, vivid picture in a reader's mind. Avoid repetitive words, such as "refer back," "repeat again," "personal opinion," "past experience," and "each and every."

REAL WORLD ADVICE | **Make Concrete Nouns Specific**

In the workplace, concrete nouns in an abstract sentence can cause confusion and misunderstanding. In fact, it may even make you appear less than competent! Compare these two sentences:

Concrete nouns in abstract sentence—The boy went shopping and spent a lot of money.
Concrete nouns with specific words—John went to the Williamsburg Outlet Mall and spent $250 on four pairs of Levi's jeans.

Another consideration when writing is to use an active voice whenever possible. Passive verbs sometimes lengthen sentences, make writing more impersonal, and introduce the use of prepositional phrases. When you use **passive voice**, the subject is being acted upon. Use passive voice when you want to avoid pinpointing a specific person, problem, or issue.

Active verbs are simpler, less formal, and more precise. Active voice is the most direct way to communicate in business. When you use **active voice**, the subject is the doer of the action. Use active voice when you want your writing to be direct. Active voice makes your message clearer.

QUICK REFERENCE | **Passive Versus Active Voice**

Passive—The recommendation to end the meeting was made by Cayden Johns.
Active—Cayden Johns made the recommendation to end the meeting.
Passive—The meeting was called to order by Richard Keilman.
Active—Richard Keilman called the meeting to order.
Passive—The dancers were invited to perform by the National Honor Society.
Active—The National Honor Society invited the dancers to perform.

Today's workplace challenges employees to communicate across cultures, genders, and age groups. Be respectful and sensitive to the feelings of the recipients of your message and avoid **biased language**—language which stereotypes or unfairly categorizes an individual or a group of people. Avoid language that evokes stereotypes. Effective communication means you must express yourself clearly, professionally, and with regard for the needs and sensitivities of your audience.

QUICK REFERENCE	Gender-Biased Versus Unbiased Language
businessman	businessperson
congressman	member of Congress
manmade	artificial
waitress	wait staff
manpower	workforce, personnel
right hand man	assistant, helper
common man	ordinary person, average person

Positive language helps to build goodwill. When you use positive language in your communication, you are emphasizing what can be done. When you use negative language, you are emphasizing what cannot be done. Negative language can cause confusion and hurt feelings, which can sometimes cause conflict and low morale.

QUICK REFERENCE | **Negative Versus Positive Language**

Negative—Your damaged smartphone has not been returned.
Positive—You will receive your new smartphone once we receive your damaged one.
Negative—We do not have an appointment available until a week from Friday.
Positive—We have an appointment available on Friday, November 12.
Negative—Do not walk on the grass.
Positive—Please walk on the sidewalk.

Revising Your Writing

Revise, edit, and proofread. Once you are comfortable with your first draft, you now begin the revising step. When you **revise**, you are checking to see if the document addresses its purpose and the required supporting information is included. When you **edit**, you are checking for clarity and understanding. When you **proofread**, you are checking for grammar, spelling, and punctuation errors.

Relying on your spelling and grammar check software programs is not sufficient. Many words can be missed that are spelled correctly but are used in the incorrect context or have a different meaning.

QUICK REFERENCE	Commonly Misunderstood Words
accept—to agree or receive	except—to exclude
affect—to influence	effect—result
compliment—to praise	complement—to make complete
formerly—in the past	formally—with official authorization
here—at the present time	hear—to listen
past—of an earlier time	passed—to go by or elapsed
principal—head, main	principle—rule
stationary—standing still	stationery—letterhead or writing material
who's—contraction for "who is"	whose—possessive form of "who"
whether—a choice between alternatives	weather—the state of the atmosphere
your—possessive form of "you"	you're—contraction for "you are"

Try to allow time between writing a document and proofreading. An error-free document conveys the message that you care and are competent. Proofread documents very carefully. Proofread for consistency in usage, facts, and format. Once the document is sent and read, the impression has been created.

In the following exercise you will learn to write in an active voice. Remember that writing in an active voice makes your message clearer.

MODULE 1

BC01.01 To Identify Differences Between Active and Passive Voice

a. From the Start screen or desktop, point to **the bottom-right** corner of the screen. The Charms will be displayed on the right side of the screen. Click the **Search** charm. Click inside the **search** box at the top of the page. Type Word.

b. Click **Word 2013** in the search results. The Word Start screen displays.

c. Click **Open Other Documents**. Double-click **Computer**, and then navigate to where your student data files are located, click **bc01ws01ActiveVoice**, and then click **Open**.

d. Click the **FILE** tab, and save the file in the location where you are saving your files with the name bc01ws01ActiveVoice_LastFirst, using your last name and first name.

e. Revise each sentence so that it reflects an active voice instead of a passive voice. An example has been provided for you.

f. Save your document and close Word.

Prepare Written Messages

Businesses use some form of written communication daily to interact with their employees, customers, and clients. Written communication allows you to spend more time on the content and wording of the message. Before sending any form of written message consider the following:

- A written message is permanent whether it is an e-mail, letter, memo, or text message. You cannot take it back.
- Written messages lack the nonverbal cues and body language so the message may be perceived differently than it was intended.
- The exchange back and forth between written channels can be more tedious and time consuming. Make sure your written message is clear and concise to avoid excessive exchanges for clarification.
- Many first impressions are made through written means. Often your first contact with a company is your resume and cover letter.

Letters, memos, reports, and e-mail are considered to be the foremost means of sending and receiving written information. E-mail is discussed in the digital communication section.

Preparing Letters

With the ongoing use of digital technology, e-mail has become the most popular channel to send internal and external written messages. However, a well-written letter is still one of the most effective ways to get your message across and is used when (1) formality and sensitivity is important, (2) confidentiality is needed, or (3) a permanent or legal record is needed.

A business letter is usually typed in one of three styles. Table 2 explains the differences among the three styles. Figure 6 shows an example of each style.

Letter Style	Description
Block	Entire letter is left-aligned and single spaced.
Modified block	Body of the letter is left-aligned and single spaced. Date, closing, and signature block are left-aligned slightly to the right of center.
Semi-block	Identical to modified block except each body paragraph is indented by ½".

Table 2 Business letter styles

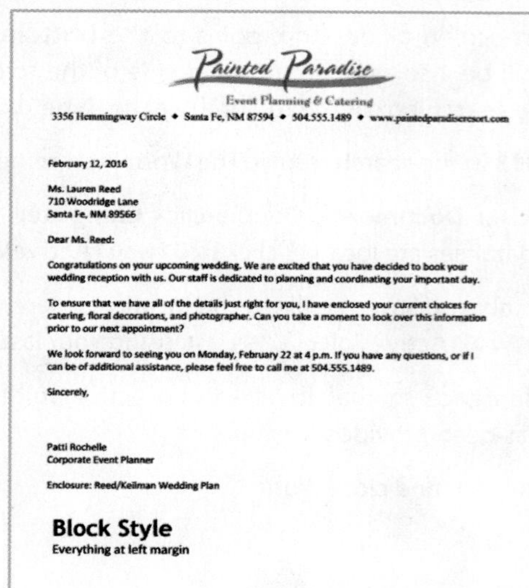
Painted Paradise
Event Planning & Catering
3356 Hemmingway Circle ◆ Santa Fe, NM 87594 ◆ 504.555.1489 ◆ www.paintedparadiseresort.com

February 12, 2016

Ms. Lauren Reed
710 Woodridge Lane
Santa Fe, NM 89566

Dear Ms. Reed:

Congratulations on your upcoming wedding. We are excited that you have decided to book your wedding reception with us. Our staff is dedicated to planning and coordinating your important day.

To ensure that we have all of the details just right for you, I have enclosed your current choices for catering, floral decorations, and photographer. Can you take a moment to look over this information prior to our next appointment?

We look forward to seeing you on Monday, February 22 at 4 p.m. If you have any questions, or if I can be of additional assistance, please feel free to call me at 504.555.1489.

Sincerely,

Patti Rochelle
Corporate Event Planner

Enclosure: Reed/Keilman Wedding Plan

Block Style
Everything at left margin

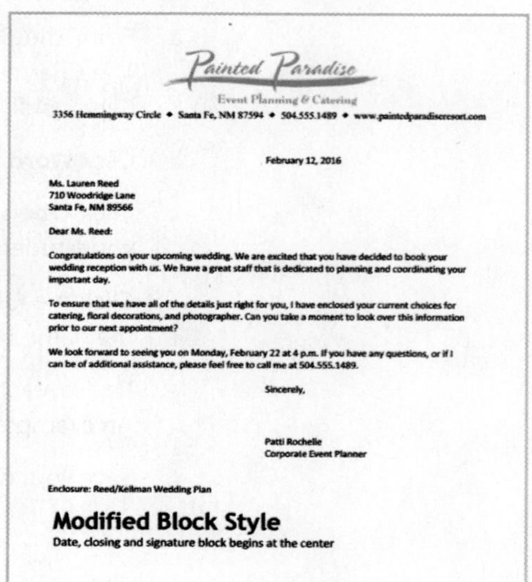
Painted Paradise
Event Planning & Catering
3356 Hemmingway Circle ◆ Santa Fe, NM 87594 ◆ 504.555.1489 ◆ www.paintedparadiseresort.com

February 12, 2016

Ms. Lauren Reed
710 Woodridge Lane
Santa Fe, NM 89566

Dear Ms. Reed:

Congratulations on your upcoming wedding. We are excited that you have decided to book your wedding reception with us. We have a great staff that is dedicated to planning and coordinating your important day.

To ensure that we have all of the details just right for you, I have enclosed your current choices for catering, floral decorations, and photographer. Can you take a moment to look over this information prior to our next appointment?

We look forward to seeing you on Monday, February 22 at 4 p.m. If you have any questions, or if I can be of additional assistance, please feel free to call me at 504.555.1489.

Sincerely,

Patti Rochelle
Corporate Event Planner

Enclosure: Reed/Kellman Wedding Plan

Modified Block Style
Date, closing and signature block begins at the center

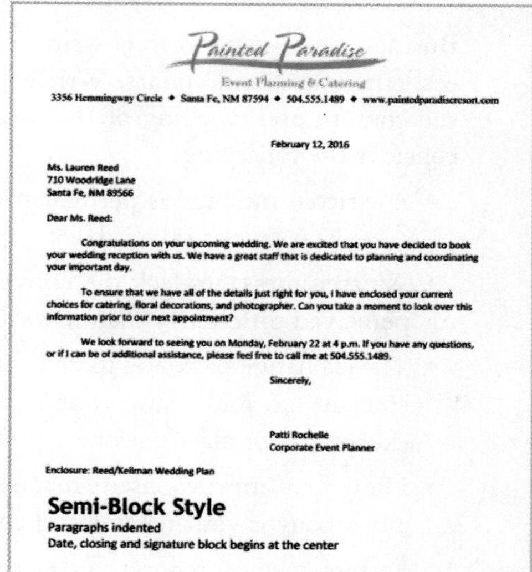
Painted Paradise
Event Planning & Catering
3356 Hemmingway Circle ◆ Santa Fe, NM 87594 ◆ 504.555.1489 ◆ www.paintedparadiseresort.com

February 12, 2016

Ms. Lauren Reed
710 Woodridge Lane
Santa Fe, NM 89566

Dear Ms. Reed:

Congratulations on your upcoming wedding. We are excited that you have decided to book your wedding reception with us. We have a great staff that is dedicated to planning and coordinating your important day.

To ensure that we have all of the details just right for you, I have enclosed your current choices for catering, floral decorations, and photographer. Can you take a moment to look over this information prior to our next appointment?

We look forward to seeing you on Monday, February 22 at 4 p.m. If you have any questions, or if I can be of additional assistance, please feel free to call me at 504.555.1489.

Sincerely,

Patti Rochelle
Corporate Event Planner

Enclosure: Reed/Keilman Wedding Plan

Semi-Block Style
Paragraphs indented
Date, closing and signature block begins at the center

Figure 6 Letter styles

When formatting a business letter, you have the option to use either mixed or open punctuation. In **mixed punctuation**, you place a colon after the salutation and a comma after the complimentary closing. In **open punctuation**, you do not use any punctuation after the salutation or the complimentary closing. Your company may have a preference on which style it requires.

Most companies have a preprinted letterhead. You can create the same visual appeal using a computer. Computer software programs have made it easy to create personalized letterhead. Your personalized letterhead should include your basic contact information: name, address, telephone number, and website information.

REAL WORLD ADVICE **Developing a Template**

Many businesses have developed in-house templates. To save time and for consistency, consider building a template for a letterhead, memos, agendas, reports, and meeting minutes. Once you have created these documents, saving as a template is easy using Microsoft Word.

Correct letter components and spacing need to be used in business letters. A typical business letter has the following components: sender's address, date, inside address, salutation, body, complimentary closing, signature block, and reference notations. When appropriate, optional components are included. Figure 7 is an example of the components of a letter and spacing. You will find various sources which may have different spacing suggestions.

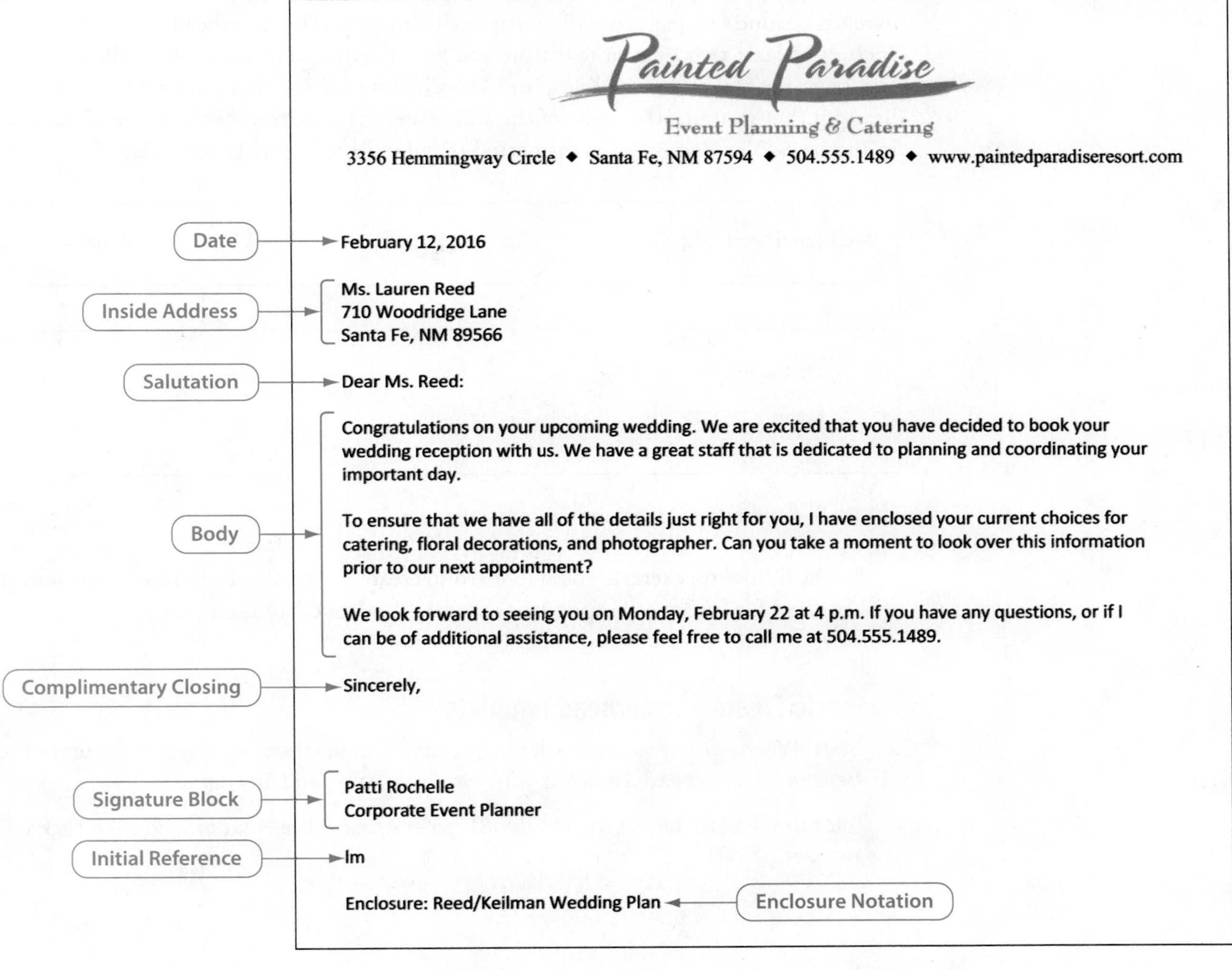
Painted Paradise
Event Planning & Catering
3356 Hemmingway Circle ◆ Santa Fe, NM 87594 ◆ 504.555.1489 ◆ www.paintedparadiseresort.com

February 12, 2016

Ms. Lauren Reed
710 Woodridge Lane
Santa Fe, NM 89566

Dear Ms. Reed:

Congratulations on your upcoming wedding. We are excited that you have decided to book your wedding reception with us. We have a great staff that is dedicated to planning and coordinating your important day.

To ensure that we have all of the details just right for you, I have enclosed your current choices for catering, floral decorations, and photographer. Can you take a moment to look over this information prior to our next appointment?

We look forward to seeing you on Monday, February 22 at 4 p.m. If you have any questions, or if I can be of additional assistance, please feel free to call me at 504.555.1489.

Sincerely,

Patti Rochelle
Corporate Event Planner

lm

Enclosure: Reed/Keilman Wedding Plan

Figure 7 Components of a letter

QUICK REFERENCE	Components of a Business Letter

Sender's address—Often in the letterhead. If not in the letterhead, include the sender's address at the top, one line above the date. Include the address, city, and zip code.
Date—This should be the date the letter is written. Write out the month, day, and year. For example: October 27, 2016.
Inside address—Shows the name and address of the recipient.
Salutation—Use the name and title from the inside address. Follow with a colon (unless using open punctuation).
Body—The main message.
Complimentary closing—The letter ending, followed by a comma (unless using open punctuation). Usually in the form of "Sincerely," but other possibilities include "Respectfully," "Respectfully Yours," and "Sincerely Yours."
Signature block—Two to four lines below the complimentary closing, followed by your typed name; may include your position.
Reference Notations—These include such items as initials, enclosures, and copies.

When possible, limit the length of your letters to one page. However, when a letter extends beyond one page, use plain paper that matches the letterhead in quality and color. Include at least two lines of text from the final paragraph of the body of the letter on the last page with the closing lines, and identify the second and succeeding pages with a heading that contains the name of the addressee, the page number, and the date, as shown in Figure 8. The document is formatted to coincide with the letter style.

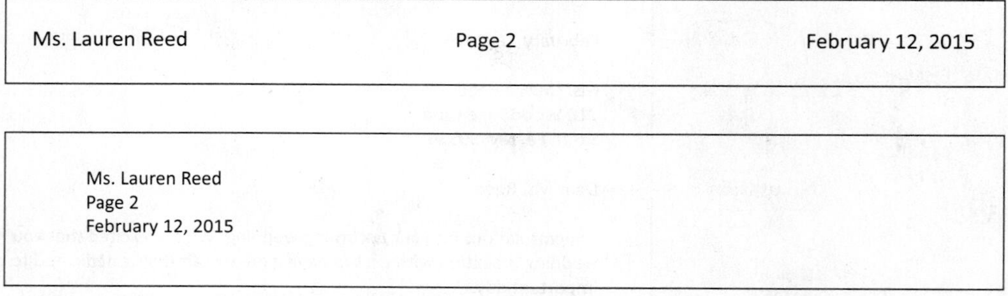

Figure 8 Formatting second and subsequent pages

In the following exercise you will learn to create a company letterhead. This letterhead will be used for future correspondence so it will be saved as a template.

BC01.02 To Create a Letterhead Template

a. Start **Word**, create a new blank document, and then save your document as bc01ws01Letterhead_LastFirst, using your last name and first name.

b. Click the **INSERT** tab, in the Header & Footer group, click **Header**, and then click **Edit Header**.

c. Click the **INSERT** tab, and then in the Illustrations group, click **Pictures**. Navigate to the location of your student data files. Click **bc01ws01EventPlanningLogo** and then click **Insert**. The logo is inserted in the document in the position of the cursor.

d. With the logo selected, on the **FORMAT** tab, in the Size group, click in the **Shape Height** box, type 1 and then press Enter.

e. With the logo still selected, click the **HOME** tab, and then in the Paragraph group, click **Center**.

f. Press Enter. Type 3356 Hemmingway Circle. Press spacebar twice.

g. Click the **INSERT** tab, in the Symbols group, click **Symbol**, and then click **More Symbols**. In the Symbol dialog box, click the **Symbols** tab if necessary. Select the **Font** arrow, and then select **Symbol**. Type 168 in the **Character code** box, and then click **Insert**. A black diamond symbol will be inserted into your document. Click **Close** to close the dialog box.

h. Press spacebar twice. Type Santa Fe, NM 87594.

i. Press spacebar twice and, following step g, insert the same symbol.

j. Press spacebar twice and type 504.555.1489.

k. Press spacebar twice and, following step g, insert the same symbol.

l. Press spacebar twice and type www.paintedparadiseresort.com. Save your work.

m. Next you want to save your letterhead as a template. Click the **FILE** tab, and then click **Save As**. Double-click **Computer**. Click the **Save as type** arrow and select **Word Template.** Name the template bc01ws01LetterheadTemplate_LastFirst. Navigate to the location where you are saving your files and then click **Save**. Close Word.

Composing Memorandums

A **memorandum** (memo) is used to communicate information internally. However, it may be used to communicate with groups or individuals externally. A memo, similar to an e-mail or letter, provides a written record and it is used for a number of purposes. A memo may be used to communicate company updates or policy changes, address internal issues, or distribute any company information that the company deems necessary to put in a permanent record.

A memo is single-spaced and contains a heading with four basic parts: date, to, from, and subject. The subject line should be a statement that captures the content. The memo does not have any complimentary closing lines as does a letter. An example of the proper format for a memo is shown in Figure 9.

Event Planning & Catering

3356 Hemmingway Circle ◆ Santa Fe, NM 87594 ◆ 504.555.1489 ◆ www.paintedparadiseresort.com

Memo

To: Painted Paradise Event Planning Group

From: Patti Rochelle, Events Coordinator

Date: May 13, 2016

Re: Putts for Paws Charity Golf Tournament

Heading

Painted Paradise Golf Resort and Spa is once again sponsoring the Annual Red Bluff Putts for Paws Golf Tournament with this year's proceeds benefiting the Santa Fe Animal Center. The success of this fundraiser will be determined by the participation and support of our community partners. As a valued member of the Event Planning staff at Painted Paradise, you are an employee I can count on to promote the event and to solicit participation from the community. So that you may be well informed and able to answer questions from interested parties, this memo provides basic details on activities and sponsorship opportunities.

The tournament, beginning at noon on July 30, promises a full afternoon of special events and exciting competition. Participants can enjoy a warm-up session with our own Red Bluff Golf Pro, John Schilling, as well as chipping and putting contests. Animals from the Santa Fe Animal Center, available for adoption, will be on hand to visit. A silent auction and raffle will round out the day. Of course, the tournament would not be complete without our highly acclaimed dessert buffet, with prized selections from Indigo5! Painted Paradise Golf Resort and Spa has prepared for you a fun-filled day at the resort!

Body

We believe in giving back to the community. We are also certain that our community partners and past donors share our commitment to support such worthwhile causes as the Santa Fe Animal Center. We invite our community partners to participate in the event by sponsoring a golf cart, a hole on the golf course, or a course flagstick. We also invite participation in the form of individual or corporate golf teams. Pricing details on all of those opportunities are given below.

- Individual Player - $200
- Team of Four - $550
- Corporate Team of Four - $850 (includes hole sponsorship)
- Cart Sponsor (Logo/brand displayed on cart) - $2000
- Hole Sponsor (Logo/brand displayed on a course tee) - $500
- Flag Sponsor (Logo/brand displayed on a course flagstick) - $500

We look forward to a fun-filled tournament—an activity that truly gives back to our community while also enabling us to connect with those who share our commitment. Sponsorship and participation in the Putts for Paws Tournament will allow us to promote local businesses while encouraging donations to the Animal Center and adoption of animals to loving homes. I appreciate your involvement and know that I can count on you to support the effort in any way you are asked.

Figure 9 Components of a memo

In the past an interoffice memo was delivered either by putting it in the recipient's office mailbox or sending it via a reusable interoffice envelope. Today the majority of internal information is being sent via e-mail, as an e-mail attachment, or as a post on the company's intranet site.

In the following exercise you will use the letterhead template you created and modify it to create a memo template. Saving this as a template will ensure that others do not save over your work.

MODULE 1

BC01.03 To Create a Memo Template

a. Start **Word**, click **Open Other Documents**, double-click **Computer**, navigate to the location where you are saving your files, and then double-click **bc01ws01LetterheadTemplate_LastFirst.** This is the template you created in the previous section.

b. Click the **FILE** tab, click **Save As**. Double-click **Computer**. Click the **Save as type** arrow and select **Word Template.** Name the template bc01ws01MemoTemplate_LastFirst. Navigate to the location where you are saving your files and then click **Save**.

c. Press Ctrl + Home on the keyboard to go to the top of your template.

d. Press Enter and type Memo.

e. Press Enter. Type To: and then apply Bold to the text To but not the colon. Press Enter and type From: and again apply Bold to the text From and not the colon.

f. Press Enter. Type Date: and then apply Bold to the text Date but not the colon. Press Enter and type Re: and again apply Bold to the text Re and not the colon.

g. Double-click the text **Memo** to select the text. On the **HOME** tab, in the **Font** group, click the **Font Size** arrow, and then select **22**. With the text still selected, apply **Bold**.

h. Save your work and close Word.

Writing Reports

Business reports are generally longer in format than memos or letters. There are two categories of business reports. Informal reports are short reports written for internal job-related purposes. Formal reports are longer reports written to assist with making better business decisions. Most of these reports will provide an analysis of statistical and trend data and make recommendations.

When transmitting a report, the business letter or memo is used as an introduction for the business report. Some of the most frequently written reports include the feasibility study, the annual report, the strategic plan, the marketing plan, and the business proposal.

All business reports, informal and formal, include four basic sections. Formal reports may include additional sections, such as a title page, table of contents, executive summary, findings, and appendix. The four basic sections are as follows:

- Introduction—The introduction provides an overview of the contents delineated in the body of the report. It includes the report's purpose and problem statement.
- Body—The body includes the key elements.
- Conclusion or summary—The conclusion or summary provides readers with a summary of the major findings.
- Recommendations—The recommendations are suggestions for improvement or changes.

For academic reports, a 2" top margin is recommended for the first page, and all subsequent pages should have a 1" top margin. A 1" side and bottom margin should be used. However, if the report is to be bound, increase the left margin by ½". Today, the ongoing trend for business reports is to use a 1" top and bottom margin and to single-space reports with a double-space between paragraphs. Because of the advancements in productivity software, in some cases businesses are formatting documents to look more like typeset publications with at least two columns of text.

Several levels of headings are used and formatted to indicate the level of importance. When headings are used effectively, they help the reader to better understand the message. They are used to direct the reader from one section to the next. Microsoft Word has several built-in styles that can be used to assist the writer with formatting different heading levels. As with a traditional outline or an organizational chart, headings in a report are written in a tiered structure. The major headings are formatted to draw more attention than the minor headings.

Brief headings are used to capture the reader's attention. Questions may be used. All headings should be parallel in structure. If questions are used, questions should be used for each heading.

REAL WORLD ADVICE | **Ethical Considerations**

Sometimes plagiarized text and fraudulent data enter the communication process. If you are required to conduct research, do not forget to cite your sources. When quoting or paraphrasing the ideas of another person, cite the source using the proper documentation.

Documenting sources demonstrates honesty, enhances credibility, substantiates the accuracy and reliability of the information, and, most importantly, protects the writer from being accused of plagiarism.

In the following exercise you will learn to format a formal report using Styles in Microsoft Word. In addition you will add a cover page.

BC01.04 To Format a Report Using Styles

a. Start **Word**, click **Open Other Documents**, double-click **Computer**, navigate to the location you are saving your student data files, click **bc01ws01FormattingReport** and then click **Open**.

b. Click the **FILE** tab, and save the file in the location where you are saving your files with the name bc01ws01FormattingReport_LastFirst, using your last name and first name.

c. Click the **INSERT** tab, and then click **Cover Page** in the Pages group. Click the cover page you want to use in the Built-in gallery. Click the document title, and then type Conducting Business in Sweden. Type your name in the subtitle or author placeholder. Delete any unused placeholders if necessary.

d. Click the **HOME** tab, and then select the report heading **Conducting Business in Sweden** on the first page of the body content. Click **More** in the Styles group, and then click **Title**. Center the title on the page.

e. Continue selecting headings and applying the following styles:

Swedish Culture	Heading 1
Status	Heading 2
Management Style	Heading 2
The Business Meeting	Heading 1
Time	Heading 2
Dress	Heading 2
Introductions and Greetings	Heading 2
Recommendations and Conclusions	Heading 1

f. Click the **REVIEW** tab, and then in the **Proofing** group, click **Spelling & Grammar**. Correct any misspelled words and grammatical errors.

g. Save the report and close Word.

Apply Strategies for Writing Messages

Whether you are writing a letter, memo, or e-mail message, you should consider how well your message will be received. Is it a positive message, neutral message, or will it encounter resistance and be a negative message? As you write messages, you will need to decide whether a direct or indirect approach would be your best option.

When you use the **direct approach**, the main idea is written first followed by the explanation. This approach anticipates no resistance. Most receivers prefer this approach as they are in a hurry and want to get to the main point right away. The direct approach is better for positive and neutral messages.

When you use the **indirect approach**, a buffer—explanation—is written first. The indirect approach is better for negative news.

QUICK REFERENCE | **Direct Versus Indirect Approach**

Direct approach—As of March 1, our hotel rates will increase by 10%.
Indirect approach—We value your business with Painted Paradise Golf Resort and Spa. We are looking forward to booking your next business event with us. As of March 1, our hotel rates will increase by 10%.

Conveying Positive and Neutral Messages

Positive news messages convey positive and pleasant information. Because the receiver is glad to accept the message, the direct approach is used. The positive news is written in the opening paragraph. Examples of positive news messages include acknowledging favorable requests and orders; expressing goodwill, such as letters of appreciation, congratulations, and condolences; and accepting employment offers.

REAL WORLD ADVICE | **Goodwill Messages**

Traditionally, handwritten notes of appreciation, congratulations, and condolences are considered more personable. When writing handwritten notes, make sure your handwriting is legible.

When responding to positive and neutral news messages, state the response in the opening sentence. A prompt response improves your chances of increasing your customer base. The major purpose is to increase contact. The way you handle a favorable request will determine how you will handle future requests. Follow these suggested steps in providing positive news:

1. State the positive news.
2. Confirm the details of the request or order.
3. End with a positive closing. Offer to give additional assistance and end with a goodwill closing.

Composing Negative Messages

Writing negative messages is difficult because negative news has the tendency to stand out. Consistent discussions very seldom take place about wonderful things, but there are usually ongoing discussions about things that are not going well. To deal with those negative messages, sensitivity is paramount. Use the indirect approach to present the bad news slowly and maintain the reader's attention until an explanation has been provided.

Communicating negative news—telling customers that a request cannot be granted, a product is being recalled, rejecting a job candidate, or terminating an employee—requires skill. The reader will not be pleased with the message. To deliver the negative news diplomatically, use the indirect approach and passive voice. The indirect approach helps to reduce the bluntness of the bad news, and passive voice focuses the bad news on the action instead of the person. The overall goal is to write a response so that the reader will desire to continue interacting with you and your company. The following steps will help you to frame negative news messages:

1. Start with a friendly, buffer paragraph. Acknowledge the facts but avoid putting the bad news in the very first sentence. Show empathy and respect.
2. Explain why you have to say no. Provide your reason for saying no, and emphasize what can be done. Be fair. Cite the company's policy and the benefits to the reader.
3. Provide a positive closing. Offer an alternative solution, if possible.

Writing Persuasive Messages

In persuasive messages you try to convince the reader to change an attitude, belief, or to take an action. Some examples of persuasive messages might be to donate to a charity, vote for a political candidate, agree to an idea for a new product or procedure, or to accept an application for employment.

For persuasive messages, you need to take the same steps to writing as you take for all messages; planning, writing, and revising. As you are trying to convince your audience to take a certain action, more time in the planning stage may be needed. Analyzing your audience, determining a clear purpose, and gathering the information needed to make a compelling argument is essential.

In the writing stage you need to appeal to the audience by using the "You" attitude. The reader wants to know how taking your action will benefit them. Writing with the "You" attitude requires you to keep the reader's needs and wants into focus.

QUICK REFERENCE	Writing with the "You" Attitude

We Attitude—We cannot process your return until we get a copy of your sales receipt.
You Attitude—So that you can receive a prompt refund, please enclose a copy of your sales receipt.

The indirect approach is often used when writing persuasive messages and can even be translated into a four-step AIDA method—attention, interest, desire, and action. It is a common method used in marketing.

1. Attention—Grab the reader's attention by writing an engaging opening sentence or asking a question. This prepares your audience for what you are going to say about your main idea—the problem, product, or service.
2. Interest—Present the benefits to the reader.
3. Desire—Help the reader form the impression that they want to receive the benefits you are suggesting. Provide detailed information to eliminate resistance.
4. Action—Issue the call to action that is the point of your persuasive message and provide the information needed to take the action.

Once you have your message written, you will need to proofread and revise as needed. It is a good idea to have someone who knows your audience look over your message. Remember that persuasive messages are written to individuals who may be resistant to your idea, product, or service. Ask yourself: (1) Is my message clear and concise? (2) Is my message positive and polite? (3) Did I present all of the facts correctly so that I have established credibility? (4) Have I provided evidence?

In the following exercise you will learn to use the "You" attitude in your writing. The reader wants to know what benefit taking an action will do for them, so take this approach to writing persuasive messages.

BC01.05 To Write Using the You Attitude

a. Start **Word**, click **Open Other Documents**, double-click **Computer**, navigate to the location of your student data files, click **bc01ws01YouAttitude** and then click **Open**.

b. Click the **FILE** tab, and save the file in the location where you are saving your files with the name bc01ws01YouAttitude_LastFirst, using your last name and first name.

c. Revise each sentence so that it reflects a "You" attitude instead of a "We" attitude. An example has been provided for you.

d. Save your document and close Word.

Understand How Digital Communication is Transforming the Workplace

The workplace has become more mobile and global. New employees entering the workforce are bringing and demanding tremendous change in regard to their expectations of how to use digital technology in the workplace. They expect to use technology to communicate, collaborate, and connect, as shown in Figure 10.

Figure 10 Digital technologies

Digital communication is the exchange of information between a sender and receiver through a channel of transmission that is digital. Digital communication involves oral or written communication, or a combination of both. Digital technologies are fast and easy, and they are opening up new avenues for many businesses.

Managing E-mail

E-mail has become the primary channel of business communication. Although other digital communication tools are now readily available, it is predicted that e-mail will remain the primary tool for the next few years. E-mail is quick, convenient, efficient, and inexpensive.

It is important that your e-mail is professional, as it represents both you and the company. Carelessly written e-mail has resulted in misunderstandings, public relation nightmares, and many lawsuits. One of the biggest problems with e-mail messages is the quickness of sending off a reply and not taking the time to make sure the tone of the e-mail is what you are intending.

E-mail provides a permanent record and can be used in legal matters. Do not write anything that you would not want others to see. When you send an e-mail, you have no idea where the electronic trail may end up.

E-mail should not be a substitute for face-to-face conversations or telephone calls when one of these options would be a better communication channel. E-mail can be appropriate for distributing information or positive news. E-mail should never be used for negative, confidential, or sensitive messages, such as performance reviews or employee disciplinary action.

REAL WORLD ADVICE | **Subject Lines in E-mail**

The subject line is often the first indication an e-mail recipient has about the importance of your e-mail message. If you want to ensure that your e-mail is read, make sure the subject line is clear and descriptive.

Ineffective Subject Line—Quarterly Report
Effective Subject Line—Business Technology—Quarter 1 Report

Consider the following e-mail guidelines as you create messages in the workplace:

- Know your company's e-mail policy and adhere to it.
- Do not use your work e-mail for personal matters.
- Use a descriptive subject line.
- Do not overuse High Importance.
- Use capital letters cautiously. E-mail etiquette considers typing in all capital letters as shouting.
- Do not reply in anger.
- Make sure the message is pertinent for all recipients when sending a message to a group.
- Avoid texting-style writing and slang. For example, do not use "u" for "you" or emoticons.

CONSIDER THIS | **E-mail Privacy—Is There Really Such a Thing?**

Some e-mail is confidential, such as to your attorney. Others are subject to "sunshine" laws that allow a public official to disclose your e-mail to a third party without your consent. Some companies have mandatory footers for e-mails deemed confidential or work product. In what kinds of situations should such a footer be included in your e-mail? What setting in e-mail could you use to indicate the message's privacy level? Should e-mail subject to a sunshine law warn respondents of that fact?

In the following exercise you will improve ineffective e-mail subject lines so that they catch the reader's attention. Remember that the subject line may make the difference on whether the reader opens the e-mail immediately or sends it to junk mail.

BC01.06 To Write Effective E-mail Subject Lines

a. Start **Word**, click **Open Other Documents**, double-click **Computer**, navigate to the location of your student data files, click **bc01ws01EmailSubjectLines** and then click **Open**.

b. Click the **FILE** tab, and save the file in the location where you are saving your files with the name bc01ws01EmailSubjectLines_LastFirst, using your last name and first name.

c. Revise each subject line so that it the subject line is more specific and will catch the reader's attention.

d. Save your document and close Word.

Using Instant Messaging and Text Messaging

Text and instant messaging have been around for a while, but the rapid increase in the use of mobile devices has caused an explosion in the number of text and instant messages for both personal and business use. More and more individuals are using these as a speedy communication channel for short messages.

Instant messaging (IM) uses a client, such as Skype, Yahoo! Messenger, or Microsoft Lync to send instant messages over the Internet. Both parties must have accounts with the IM service. Individuals are able to communicate in real-time. It is good for an immediate back and forth exchange provided the individual you wish to IM is online. Some companies have embraced the use of this technology and yet others may discourage or ban it due to the fear of company information being shared over public networks.

Text messaging (SMS) does not have the constraints of both parties needing the same proprietary client. All you need is a mobile device capable of sending and receiving text messages. Text messaging is being used in companies to advertise products and services, improve customer service, and to advertise promotional offers.

Text and instant messages, however, can be a factor in litigation and investigations. You will want to keep this in mind when using these communication channels in the workplace.

REAL WORLD ADVICE — Text and Instant Messaging—Professional Guidelines for the Workplace

Before sending an instant message or text message, remember that these messages are a direct reflection on you and your place of work. Make sure your messages are clear and concise and have a professional tone. Use proper punctuation and capitalization. Edit and proofread before sending the message. Avoid the use of acronyms and text abbreviations. Save those for your personal messages.

Working with Blogs

A **blog** is a website that has the look and feel of a journal. Posts are arranged in reverse chronological order with the newest posted at the top. When first introduced, it was typical to have one author for a particular blog. We now often see multiple individuals authoring a blog site.

Blogging has become more critical to businesses. Blogs are used both internally and externally. Internally, blogs can be used to allow employees an opportunity to voice their opinion, share expertise, or to collaborate on team projects. For example, a team blog could be set up to put all team communications in one location. This would allow the blog to be an organizational tool, where all updates, progress reports, and announcements could be shared and stored.

Externally, blogs can be a powerful branding, marketing, and public relations tool to reach customers. Many Fortune 500 companies are using blogs to get in touch with their customers. Think of how a blog can help to differentiate your products and services from other businesses', or how it could be used by human resources for recruiting.

Writing a blog should follow the same guidelines for writing as in other written channels. The message must be meaningful to the reader and encourage the reader to post comments.

Using Wikis

A **wiki** is a web page that uses online collaborative editing tools for building its content. One of the most popular and well-known wikis is the online encyclopedia Wikipedia.

Using wikis in a business setting allows employees to collaborate and participate in decision making and the exchange of ideas. Wikis have become popular as an online project management tool. Aside from project management, companies use wikis for activities, such as setting meeting agendas or posting corporate policies.

Using Podcasts

A **podcast** is an audio, video, or digital media that is distributed over the Internet to a computing device, such as a personal computer or portable media player. Individuals either go to a podcasting website to listen to the podcast, or they can download a podcast to their portable media player. Another alternative is to subscribe to Really Simple Syndication (RSS) feeds which enable your podcasting software to pull content automatically.

Businesses use podcasts to communicate with customers and with their employees. Podcasts are great for training, product launches, customer support issues such as the top FAQs, and press releases, to name just a few. Companies find that podcasts are beneficial because customers, clients, and employees are not always available at a designated time, so being able to download and listen to a podcast at their convenience is a great way to disseminate information.

Using Social Networking Sites

Today, having a social networking site is one of the best ways to stay connected. Millions of people log on to these sites daily. Thus, businesses are using social networking sites, such as Facebook, Twitter, and LinkedIn to interact with their suppliers, customers, professional contacts, and business associates. These social network sites can be accessed via computers or mobile devices.

Facebook and Twitter are being used to establish personal and professional relationships by keeping friends or customers informed of changes, such as new product lines, sale items, product recalls, and more. LinkedIn connects people with professional colleagues. The professional network you develop on LinkedIn can assist you when you are seeking employment. Additional information about LinkedIn will be discussed in Workshop 2.

Using Cloud Computing

Within recent years, computing has moved to services offered on the Internet—referred to as **cloud computing**. Figure 11 shows an example of cloud computing. Cloud computing allows users to keep files on the Internet rather than on their computer. The cloud offers new opportunities for using applications because applications, music, video, and tools for collaboration can be accessed almost anytime, anywhere, on almost any device as long as there is Internet connectivity. Microsoft's newest version of Office not only offers Microsoft Office but also website hosting, file sharing, e-mail, calendaring, instant messaging, web conferencing, Office web apps, and enhanced security features. There are also several free web applications for creating, storing, and sharing documents, spreadsheets, and presentations in the cloud, such as Google Docs and Apache OpenOffice.

Figure 11 Cloud computing

Other popular tools used to communicate are web or mobile apps. App is short for application. Web and mobile apps provide the power of the Internet with multi-touch capability. There are thousands of apps available for download. You can get apps to assist with locating the cheapest gas within a certain radius, managing your bank account, turning the lights on and off in your house, reading books, collaborating at work, and so much more.

Participating in Web Conferencing—Virtual Meetings

As technology has advanced, conferencing tools have also evolved from teleconferencing to videoconferencing to web conferencing. **Web conferencing** is an interactive way to simulate face-to-face meetings between two or more participants at different locations, using computer networks and software over the Internet as shown in Figure 12.

© Andrey_Popov/Shutterstock

Figure 12 Web conferencing

Virtual meetings are growing in popularity as alternative ways to conduct meetings. The technology to conduct virtual meetings has advanced to the point that many businesses are willing to invest in the technology needed to hold virtual meetings to save time and money. GoToMeeting and WebEx are popular web conferencing software services used for meetings. Web conferencing software is constantly improving and currently includes the ability to capture screens, chat, provide instant polling, use an electronic whiteboard, view slide presentations, and share applications.

Participating in Webinars and Webcasts

Webinars and webcasts are other ways businesses can broadcast over the Internet to an audience. A webinar occurs in real time, where the audience is interactive. Webinars attempt to simulate the experience of attending a seminar only using the Internet. Webinars usually follow an agenda in which the presenter gives a presentation or demonstration to the audience. At the end of the presentation, the audience is given the opportunity to ask questions, and can be surveyed or polled for feedback. A webcast is different because it is essentially a one-way communication over the Internet. There is no interaction with the audience. Often webcasts are pre-recorded and placed on the Internet for an individual to view at their convenience. Both webinars and webcasts are popular educational and marketing tools.

Use Effective Oral Communication Skills in the Workplace

As with written communication, effective oral communication skills are essential. A great deal of the communication that takes place in the workplace is spontaneous and informal. Take the same care with reinforcing effective oral communication skills as you do with your written skills.

Besides the informal conversations that occur in the workplace, business professionals must make telephone calls and leave voice messages; participate in meetings; and make presentations, speeches, or oral reports. With each of these forms of oral communication, effective listening is crucial. Listening was discussed earlier as part of the information in the section "Understand the Communication Process."

Participating in Informal and Formal Discussions

Whether you are engaging in informal or formal discussions, think about what you are going to say before you say it. It is easier to change what you say before you say it, than after it has been said. Differences in speaker's and audience's perceptions account for most misunderstandings and conflicts.

As you interact with your coworkers, managers, or supervisors at the water cooler, in the elevator, the corridor, or at social gatherings, be mindful of what you say and how you say it. You never know who may write a recommendation for you for a job or promotion in the future. Treat these informal discussions as an extension of your workplace.

Formal discussions generally take place during planned events, such as meetings. Because these are less casual and spontaneous, we sometimes do a better job of communicating in a more structured environment as we can prepare in advance.

Using the Telephone and Voice Mail

Businesses rely heavily on the use of the phone to conduct day-to-day operations. Many times a phone call is the first impression that a prospective customer or client has of your workplace. It is imperative that proper phone etiquette be used in order to ensure a positive business image.

In addition to landline phones, smartphones and digital voice technologies are being used to communicate. Regardless of the type of telephone technology used, business professionals need to follow some general guidelines. It is not what you say, but how you say it that matters. Use the suggestions listed below to assist you with being courteous and thoughtful when using the phone.

- When placing a call, speak clearly. Use a pleasant, friendly tone. Avoid eating and drinking while talking. Avoid using slang. Be professional.
- When receiving a call, answer promptly. Identify your department or unit and state your name. Be polite. Ask before placing a caller on hold.
- When leaving a message, repeat your name and phone number at the beginning and end of the message. Speak slowly. Leave a detailed, but brief, message.
- When taking a message, write down all of the details. Identify the caller, date and time of the call, phone number of the caller, and your name or initials.
- When using a cell phone, respect quiet zones. Remember safety. Obey cell phone policies at your workplace. Place your phone on silent during meetings.

Your voice mail greeting is just as important as your greeting when you answer the phone. It can be the first contact that someone has with you or your company. Your voice mail greeting should let the caller know who they have reached, your out-of-the-office status, when they can expect a call back, and instructions about what to do if the call is urgent.

Planning and Delivering Presentations

Presentations are an essential part of business, and they are primarily given to inform, educate or to persuade others. They can be as informal as presenting to a small departmental unit or as formal as presenting at a national conference as shown in Figure 13. When done well, oral presentations can enhance your career options, credibility, and value to an organization.

© Rawpixel/Fotolia

Figure 13 Delivering a presentation

Preparation is a key ingredient to your presentation's success. Preparing for your presentation involves the following:

1. Determine the purpose and the message. Purpose and message are not the same. The purpose is to inform, persuade, or educate. The message is what you want the audience to remember when they walk away. It will help you focus. An example of a persuasive message to a sales group may be to increase sales by 25%.
2. Analyze the audience. All audiences are different. What are their expectations? Failure to address the audience's needs will hinder your ability to get the audience to buy into your message. If you do not have personal knowledge of your audience, find someone who does. Do your research on the audience.
3. Collect information and facts. Research thoroughly. You need to be an expert, or close to it, on the material. You need to know the critical facts and information. It is not unusual to spend a considerable amount of time on this step. The bigger the presentation, the more time this may take. Make sure you have reliable information and that your facts can be documented.
4. How much interaction with the audience will be involved? Of course, the more interaction the better. But the amount of time and the number of attendees, as well as other factors will influence the amount of interaction.
5. Organize the information. At this point, you are ready to start organizing your material into a logical sequence. Make sure you have a strong introduction that will grab the audience's attention.
6. Plan your visuals. What visuals will you need to get your ideas across? Will you use presentation software, a whiteboard, a flip chart, handouts, or overhead transparencies? Visuals need to be just that—have visual meaning and not just text.
7. End with a powerful conclusion. Your conclusion should tell the audience what you want them to take away from the presentation; what they should do.

Another key ingredient to the success of your presentation is practice. Before you are ready to deliver your presentation, you need to rehearse. The biggest mistake most presenters make is to not rehearse. They read through the presentation over and over, but this is not the same as rehearsing. If you do not speak the presentation, then you have not rehearsed. Rehearse anywhere; in the car, in the shower, or in the office. It really does not matter as long as you are prepared.

Your audience will rate the effectiveness of your presentation on what they see as well as what they hear. Dress professionally for your presentation. Remember your attire is the first thing the audience will notice about you, before you even open your mouth. It will create the first impression. Make it a good one. Do not let your appearance get in the way of your presentation's message.

Body language has a huge impact on the audience and should convey a positive image. Move around; do not stand in one place. Maintain eye contact with the audience. It is recommended that you maintain eye contact with the audience 80–90% of the time you are presenting. Facial expressions and gestures play an important role in your delivery. Make sure they convey your intended meaning.

The use of your voice is another consideration. Use of pitch variation, speaking speed, and emphasis should be practiced.

Using Presentation Software

The use of presentation software, especially PowerPoint, has become the norm for many business presentations. Other popular presentation tools include Google Docs, Apple Keynote, Prezi, and Adobe Presenter. Electronic presentations are relatively easy to create. They can include text, images, animation, sound, and video. Thus, some are filled with an excess of information, poor readability, inappropriate color, meaningless graphics, clip art, animation, and copyright infringements.

To make your presentation look professional, keep your slides simple. Often, less is more. Don't be afraid to use white space on your slides. Too much text causes the slides to look overcrowded and boring.

Listed below are some guidelines to assist you with designing better slides:

- Templates and backgrounds—Presentation software comes with backgrounds and templates from which you can choose. Consider designing your own template for a personalized look and feel. Anyone who has created or viewed presentations knows the built-in templates. Choose your background carefully. The background needs to complement your topic.
- Photos and clip art—Use quality photographs not clip art. There are a variety of places to get free or inexpensive photos. Make sure your images are relevant and communicate your intended message. The use of large, full-screen graphics, if relevant, can have a high impact.
- Colors—Be conscious of colors and their effect on your audience. Colors are divided into two main categories: Cool (green, purple, and blue) and Warm (orange, yellow, and red). Cool colors work best for backgrounds. Use contrast, such as a light background with dark text, which is easier for your audience to read.
- Fonts—Use only one or two fonts styles in a presentation. Use one for the heading and one for body text. Research shows that serif fonts are harder to read when projected, therefore it is recommended that you use a sans serif font. Font size is important. A general rule of thumb for font size is 30 points or larger for a conference room. Avoid all caps except on the title slide.
- Bullet points—If you must use bullet points, make sure they represent the main idea and are not paragraphs. One of the most common complaints for using presentation software is the overuse of bullet points, or putting full sentences on the slide. If you must use bullet points, consider "chunking" your information for a better visual representation. Remember, audiences cannot read and listen well at the same time.

- Graphs and Charts—Avoid complex graphs and diagrams. Charts and graphs can be great visuals but they should be clean and simple. Remove any excess chart elements that are not needed.
- Animation—Animation can be very useful in presenting important ideas, calling attention to specific items, or for transitional purposes. However, you need to have a purpose in order for the animation to not be a distraction. When choosing an animation, in most cases you will want to use something subtle. Blinking, spinning, bouncing, and similar effects are seldom appropriate or a good choice. Balls bounce, tops spin, and lights blink; save those animation effects for those objects.

CONSIDER THIS | What is a Pecha Kucha Presentation?

A Pecha Kucha presentation is a presentation format that is based on a simple idea: 20 slides x 20 seconds. No more than 20 slides are shown for 20 seconds each. It is a format that makes presentations concise, and keeps things going along at a rapid pace. It is derived from the Japanese term for "chit chat." What challenges do you foresee in creating a Pecha Kucha presentation? When is this format appropriate to use?

In the following exercise you will revise a PowerPoint presentation. Your job will be to make the slides more visually appealing for the audience, trying to avoid bullet-heavy slides. You will apply SmartArt to a bullet list to enhance your presentation.

BC01.07 To Makeover a PowerPoint Presentation

a. Start **PowerPoint**, click **Open Other Presentations**, double-click **Computer**, navigate to the location of your student data files, click **bc01ws01Resort** and then click **Open**.

b. Click the **FILE** tab, and save the file in the location where you are saving your files with the name bc01ws01Resort_LastFirst, using your last name and first name.

c. On **Slide 1**, replace **Presenter Name** with your name.

d. Click on **Slide 2**. This slide is using a standard bullet list. To make the slide more appealing, you convert the bullet list to SmartArt. Select the bulleted text placeholder, and on the **HOME** tab, in the Paragraph group, click **Convert to SmartArt**, and then choose **More SmartArt Graphics**. In the Choose a SmartArt Graphic dialog box, click **Basic Block List**, and then click **OK**.

e. Under SMARTART TOOLS, on the DESIGN tab, in the SmartArt Styles group, click **Change Colors**, and then click **Colorful-Accent Colors**. In the SmartArt Styles group, click **More**, and then under 3-D, click **Polished**.

f. Save the presentation and close PowerPoint.

Planning and Delivering Team Presentations

You may be asked to participate in a team presentation. The general guidelines for planning and delivering a presentation still hold true. Each team member's role in developing and delivering the presentation will need to be considered. Careful coordination of the sequencing of who speaks when will be important to ensure continuity of the presentation. If a question and answer time will be part of the presentation, it will need to be determined how this will be handled.

Team presentations require more rehearsing and practice as shown in Figure 14. Team members will need to be open-minded to suggestions from other team members for improvements on their individual speaking parts.

© Monkey Business Images/Shutterstock

Figure 14 Rehearsing a team presentation

Working in Teams

Employers rank written and oral communications skills, along with teamwork skills, as one of the key skills they are looking for. The National Association of Colleges and Employers Job Outlook 2013 survey confirms this. According to the survey, the ideal candidate is a good communicator who can make decisions and solve problems while working effectively in a team.

So what makes a successful team? Successful teams have members with good communication skills. Team members are willing to collaborate and cooperate with each other to arrive at a solution. Listed below are some things that make a good team environment and keep the communication channels open:

- Team members are willing to give and accept feedback.
- Team members have good listening skills.
- Team members share information and give praise.
- Team members are aware that conflict can and will arise, but are open-minded and committed to solving the problem.
- Team members ask questions when needed.
- Team members are not competing with each other for power. They use a democratic approach of shared leadership, often rotating this among members of the team.

Teams go through stages of development. One of the most commonly used frameworks for the stages of team development is the model developed by psychologist Bruce Tuckman in the 1960s. He indicated that teams go through four stages on their way to becoming a high-performing team, and in 1977 he added a fifth stage. The stages are forming, storming, norming, performing, and adjourning.

In the forming stage, the team is beginning. Individuals have a strong desire to be accepted by the other members of the team. Team members avoid controversy and conflict at this stage. Structure is being set up as to when the team will meet and how often. It is an information gathering stage and one of harmony among team members.

The next step is the storming stage. Storming is the most difficult stage for a team, but it is necessary for healthy team development. This stage is characterized by conflict and competition as members begin to address the issues. Members may argue about the actions they should take because they are faced with ideas that are unfamiliar to them and put them outside their comfort zones. Much of their energy is focused on each other instead of achieving the goal. Politeness begins to wear off and dissension occurs. Control often becomes the primary issue. Who is going to decide what? Disagreements can be either very obvious or subtle.

When team members begin to trust one another enough to air differences, this signals readiness to work things out and move on to the next stage, which is the norming stage. At this stage, the team is beginning to trust one another, they are working on their differences, and are making a strong commitment to the team goal. Roles and responsibilities are clear and accepted, and decisions are being made by consensus.

In the performing stage, the team members have discovered and accepted each other's strengths and weaknesses, and learned what their roles are. Members are open and trusting and many good ideas are produced because they are not afraid to offer ideas and suggestions. They are comfortable using decision-making tools to evaluate the ideas, prioritize tasks, and solve problems.

The last stage is the adjourning stage. At this stage, the team is winding down as the team has accomplished its purpose. Recognition for achievement and participation takes place at this stage.

Working in virtual teams has become more common today than ever before and is on the increase. You may find yourself working in a virtual team. Team members use e-mail and teleconferencing tools to meet and make decisions. Working in a virtual team across miles and time zones may present more of a communication challenge, but the same guidelines listed previously for creating a good team environment hold true.

Concept Check

1. Explain the communication process.
2. Identify the five barriers to effective communication and give an example of each.
3. What are some tips for active listening?
4. Describe some of the challenges for communicating across cultures.
5. Explain the three steps in the writing process.
6. What is the "You Attitude" and why should you use it?
7. What is the difference between an active voice and a passive voice in writing?
8. When should you use a direct approach in your writing?
9. What is the difference between block, modified block, and semi-block letter styles?
10. What are some strategies for writing persuasive messages?
11. What are the different visual aids that can be used in presentations?
12. List three good practice presentation tips.

Key Terms

Abstract words 11
Active listening 5
Active voice 11
Barrier 8
Biased language 11
Block 14
Blog 25
Channel 4
Cloud computing 27
Communication 4
Concrete words 11
Digital communication 23
Direct approach 21
Edit 12
Hearing 5
Indirect approach 21
Listening 5
Memorandum 17
Mixed punctuation 14
Modified block 14
Nonverbal communication 6
Open punctuation 14
Passive voice 11
Podcast 26
Proofread 12
Revise 12
Semi-block 14
Stereotype 7
Web conferencing 27
Wiki 26

Visual Summary

Understand cultural differences in nonverbal communication (p. 6)

Understand the communication process (p. 4)

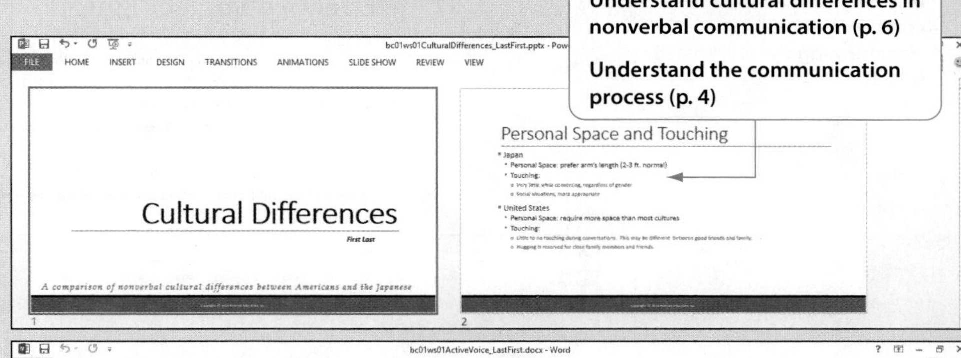

Identify differences between active and passive voice (p. 11)

Understand the business writing process (p. 9)

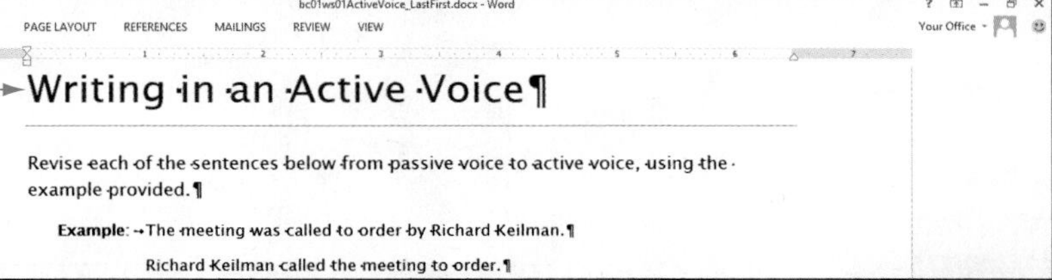

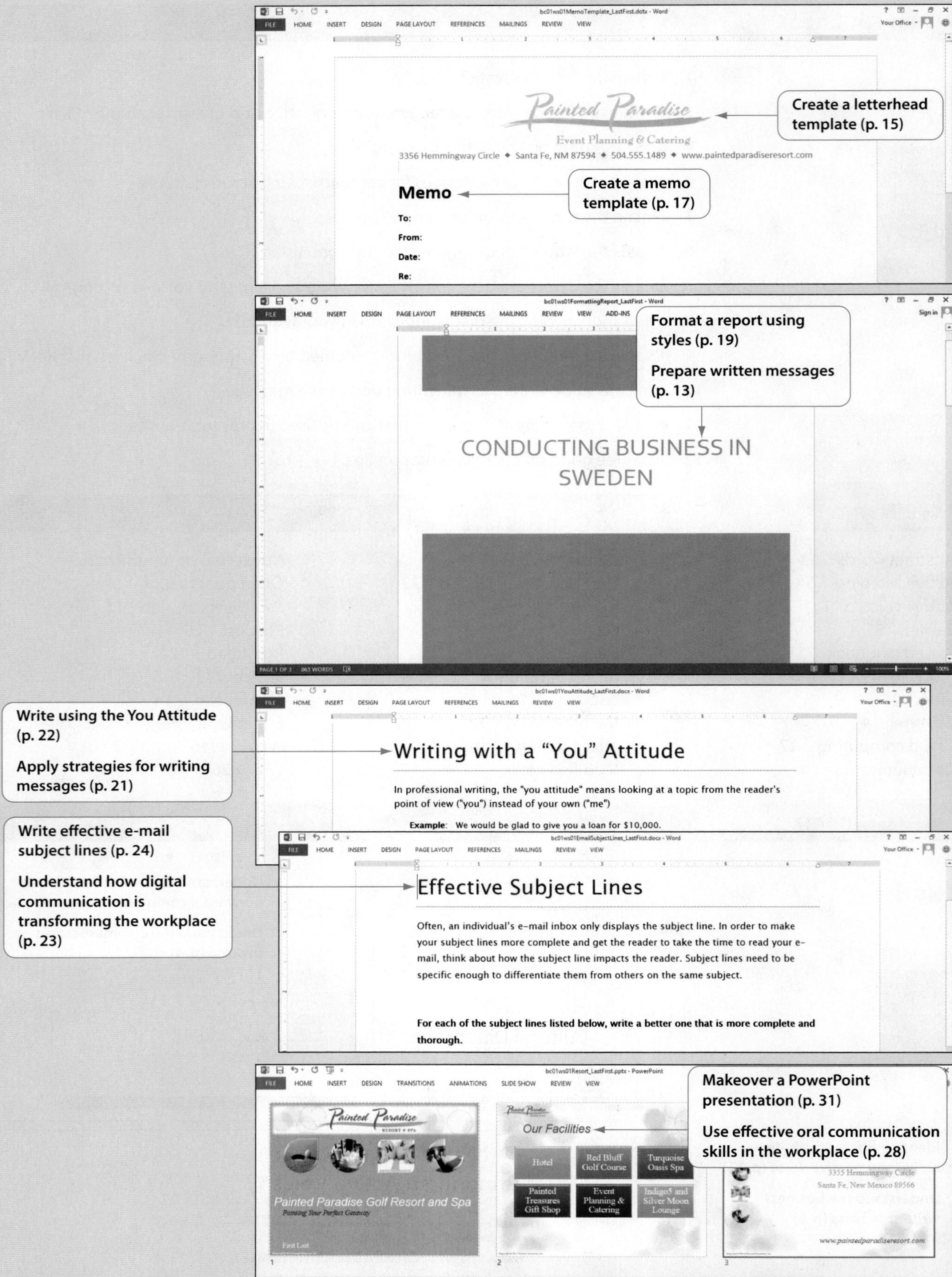

Figure 15 The communication process final

Practice 1

Student data file needed:

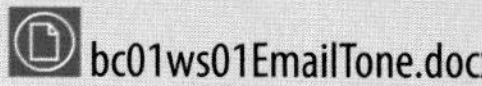
bc01ws01EmailTone.docx

You will save your file as:

bc01ws01EmailTone_LastFirst.docx

Painted Paradise Golf Resort and Spa E-mail Usage Response

An e-mail was sent to all staff at the Painted Paradise Golf Resort and Spa in regard to using the company e-mail system for personal use. The message is harsh and has the staff upset due to the tone of the message. Rewrite the e-mail taking a softer approach while still getting the message across to the reader.

a. Start **Word**, click **Open Other Documents**, double-click **Computer**, navigate to the location of your student data files, click **bc01ws01EmailTone** and then click **Open**.

b. Click the **FILE** tab, and save the file in the location where you are saving your files with the name bc01ws01EmailTone_LastFirst, using your last name and first name.

c. Review the e-mail. Pick out the areas in the message that seem overly harsh and rewrite the text using a softer tone. The message still needs to get across to the reader.

d. Click the **REVIEW** tab, and then click **Spelling & Grammar**. Correct any misspelled words and then proofread the memo.

e. Save the document and close Word.

Practice 2

Student data file needed:

bc01ws01MontgomeryWeddingConflict.docx

You will save your file as:

bc01ws01MontgomeryWeddingConflict_LastFirst.docx

Conference Center Scheduling Conflict Response

Erin Montgomery and Cayden Shultz scheduled their wedding reception at the resort for the first Saturday in March. They have a signed contract and have money down on the reception. Unfortunately, due to a family emergency in Cayden's immediate family, the reception had to be canceled. The couple is looking for another date to reschedule the wedding reception. They were hoping for the first week in June. You are unable to honor this request due to another wedding reception and event planned for that Saturday. You prepare a response to Erin, giving her the bad news and suggesting options. Use the Block style with mixed punctuation.

a. Start **Word**, click **Open Other Documents**, double-click **Computer**, navigate to the location of your student data files, click **bc01ws01MontgomeryWeddingConflict** and then click **Open**.

b. Click the **FILE** tab, and save the file in the location where you are saving your files with the name bc01ws01MontgomeryWeddingConflict_LastFirst, using your last name and first name.

c. If necessary, click **Show/Hide** in the Paragraph group to display formatting marks.

d. Press Ctrl + Home on the keyboard to go to the top of your template.

e. Press Enter twice. Type April 2, 2016.

f. Press Enter twice and type the following inside address:

Erin Montgomery
1522 Watson Lane
Las Cruces, NM 88001

g. Press [Enter] twice and type Dear Erin:

h. Press [Enter] twice and begin typing the letter. Remember that this letter is bringing disappointing news so follow the guidelines for delivering bad news. Suggest several alternatives for consideration.

i. Press [Enter] twice and add the appropriate closing and punctuation.

j. Press [Enter] four times. Type Patti Rochelle. Press [Enter] once and type Event Planning Manager.

k. Click the **REVIEW** tab, and then click **Spelling & Grammar**. Correct any misspelled words and then proofread the letter.

l. Once you have completed the letter, adjust the spacing of the letter so that it fits on the page. You may want to add some additional spacing between the letterhead and the date.

m. Save the letter and close Word.

Problem Solve 1

Student data files needed:

bc01ws01ConferencePlanning.pptx
bc01ws01ConferenceEldorado.jpg
bc01ws01ConferencePueblo.jpg

You will save your file as:

bc01ws01ConferencePlanning_LastFirst.pptx

Conference Planning Presentation

The resort needs to update its conference planning presentation for upcoming speaking engagements to promote the resort. You have been asked to make changes to the current presentation to make it more visually appealing.

a. Start **PowerPoint**, click **Open Other Presentations**, double-click **Computer**, navigate to the location of your student data files, click **bc01ws01ConferencePlanning** and then click **Open**.

b. Click the **FILE** tab, and save the file in the location where you are saving your files with the name bc01ws01ConferencePlanning_LastFirst, using your last name and first name.

c. On **Slide 1**, replace **Presenter Name** with your name.

d. Click on **Slide 2**. Select the quote and increase the font size to **40** pt. Reposition the textbox if necessary so that it is centered on the slide and looks visually appealing. Select the quotation marks at the beginning and the end of the quote and increase the font size to **66** pt. to make the quotes stand out. Select the name **Nelson Boswell** and apply italics, bold, and change the font size to **20** pt.

e. Click on **Slide 3**. In the notes section is information that needs to be addressed on the slide. You will design the slide using **SmartArt**. Choose an appropriate design for the information. Add the most important information from the notes to the SmartArt design. Remember that you want to add main ideas only. Using the SmartArt tools, make any style changes that may enhance the SmartArt.

f. Click on **Slide 4**. You will be inserting two photos from your student data files to the slide. Navigate to the location of your student data files and insert the **bc01ws01ConferenceEldorado** photo. Reposition the image so that it is under the heading The Eldorado Room. Insert the **bc01ws01ConferencePueblo** photo on the slide. Reposition the photo so that it is under the heading The Pueblo Room. Resize the photos and add any enhancements that you feel would be appropriate, such as a border style for the pictures.

g. Click on **Slide 5**. Insert a table on the slide. Select the correct number of columns and rows to add the information below. Use the Merge Cells and Split Cells options to format the table layout as suggested below. Choose an appropriate table style. Make changes to the layout for alignment as needed.

Hotel/Conference Room Rates		
Rooms Booked	**Conference Room**	**Rate**
10 – 30	Eldorado	$2,500
	Pueblo	$1,500
31 – 60	Eldorado	$2,000
61 – 90	Eldorado	$1,500
91+	Eldorado	Free

h. Click on **Slide 6**. Using the following data, create a **3D-Pie Chart**. Add the following information.

Keynote Speaker	10%
Banquet, Meals, Snacks	30%
Conference Room	15%
Entertainment	10%
Registration	5%
Technology	5%
Other	25%

i. Click the **chart** to select it. Under the CHART TOOLS, click the **DESIGN** tab. In the Chart Layouts group, click **Quick Layout**, and then click an appropriate layout for the chart.

It will be important that you have data labels visible for the audience to distinguish the costs to get an accurate analysis. If your layout has a title, delete the title as your slide title placeholder is an appropriate explanation for the chart contents. Revise the chart to make it easier to read by increasing the font size of the data labels and legend.

j. Click on **Slide 7**. Select the bullet points. On the HOME tab, in the Paragraph group, click the **Convert to SmartArt** drop down arrow. Choose a SmartArt design that would appropriately represent the information. Format the SmartArt choosing a style that would enhance the SmartArt.

k. Click on **Slide 8**. In the title placeholder, type How can WE help? Format the text so that it stands out on the slide.

l. Save the presentation and close PowerPoint.

Problem Solve 2

Student data file needed:

bc01ws01CopyrightMemo.docx

You will save your file as:

bc01ws01CopyrightMemo_LastFirst.docx

Painted Paradise Golf Resort and Spa Copyright Workshop and Luncheon

Recently some of the staff at the resort have been violating copyright guidelines when they create presentations and other print media for the resort. Copyright is an important issue that must be addressed with the staff. Lesa Martin has asked you to organize a workshop to address this issue. So that all staff will have the opportunity to attend the workshop, two workshops will be set up; one in the morning from 9–11 a.m. and another in the afternoon from 2–4 p.m. The workshops will be held one month from the current date. Stephanie Wilcox, a copyright specialist, will conduct the workshop. The title of the workshop is "**Can I Use That? Understanding Copyright.**" Draft a memo from Lesa to be distributed to all employees to persuade them to attend one of the workshops. Include information on the speaker in the memo. Use the AIDA approach to writing this memo.

a. Start **Word**, click **Open Other Documents**, double-click **Computer**, navigate to the location of your student data files, click **bc01ws01CopyrightMemo** and then click **Open**.

b. Click the **FILE** tab, and save the file in the location where you are saving your files with the name bc01ws01CopyrightMemo_LastFirst, using your last name and first name.

c. Click after the word To: and press Tab. Type Painted Paradise Staff. Click after the word From: and press Tab. Type Lesa Martin. Click after the word Date: and press Tab. Type the current date. Click after the word Re: and press Tab. Enter a catchy line to capture the reader's attention that will entice them to read further.

d. Press Enter two times. Type the memo content that describes the details of the upcoming workshops. Remember to use the AIDA method to persuade the reader to attend one of the workshops. Include the date and times, speaker information, and any other important information. In the final paragraph provide instructions for making a reservation for one of the workshops.

e. Click the **REVIEW** tab, and then click **Spelling & Grammar**. Correct any misspelled words and then proofread the memo.

f. Save the memo and close Word.

Perform 1: Perform in Your Life

Student data file needed:

bc01ws1PechaKuchaPresentation.pptx

You will save your file as:

bc01ws01PechaKuchaPresentation_LastFirst.pptx

Creating a Pecha Kucha Presentation on Tips for Presentations

One of the newest ways to show off your presentation skills is to speak at a Pecha Kucha event. Your topic choice will be "**Tips for Great Presentations**." PowerPoint has a bad reputation for causing "Death by PowerPoint." You want to help others avoid this in their business presentations. Do some research on the terms "Death by PowerPoint" and Pecha Kucha to get some additional tips to create this presentation.

Using great visuals and a minimum of text, create this presentation. Remember that you have a maximum of 20 slides which will display for only 20 seconds each while you speak. Practice, practice, and practice your presentation. The more you practice, the better it will be.

a. Start **PowerPoint**, open **bc01ws01PechaKuchaPresentation** and then save as bc01ws01PechaKuchaPresentation_LastFirst.

b. Change the template design if desired to one that you feel may better portray the topic.

c. Add your name to the title slide.

d. Design each of the 20 slides to illustrate your key points. Keep in mind that your audience will only view your slide for 20 seconds before you move on to the next key point.

e. Add notes to each of the slides as a reminder of what you plan to say.

f. Proofread your presentation for errors.

g. Practice your presentation.

h. Save your presentation and close PowerPoint.

WORKSHOP 2 | APPLYING EMPLOYMENT SEARCH STRATEGIES

OBJECTIVES

1. Prepare for your job search p. 42
2. Research employment opportunities p. 46
3. Create an application packet p. 48
4. Understand the importance of the interview p. 57
5. Prepare other employment documents p. 60
6. Understand pre-employment screening p. 65

Prepare Case

Painted Paradise Golf Resort and Spa Management Development Program Application

© Stephen Coburn/Fotolia

Your performance evaluations have been superb. Consequently, you are being recommended for the Painted Paradise Golf Resort and Spa Management Development Program (MDP). This is one of your professional goals.

You must apply! The MDP is one of the best in the industry and will be a strong training ground for your future. The program includes a combination of on-the-job training, hands-on project assignments, and an introduction to the resort's culture and values. You will have the opportunity to gain valuable management experience while rotating through a variety of roles and functional areas of business and travel in a non-threatening environment while being compensated.

If selected, you will receive a very competitive compensation and benefits package, discounts at all of the resort's venues, and educational assistance to ensure you are equipped with the prerequisite skills for a management position.

You must continue to put your best foot forward and continue to work as one of the support staff members for the Conference Center. In addition to applying for the MDP, you will continue to develop personal skills in writing employment letters and interviewing.

REAL WORLD SUCCESS

"One of the most important things I learned when looking for my first professional job out of college was to build a solid professional image by branding myself in a positive light both online and in person. Building a solid network is another key ingredient for successful job searching. I found my first job through networking."

- Erin, alumnus, Operations Manager

Student data files needed for this workshop:

 bc01ws02ProfessionalNetwork.docx
bc01ws02PlanResume.docx
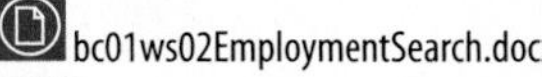 bc01ws02EmploymentSearch.docx
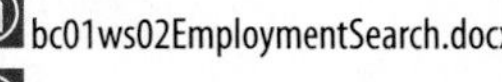
bc01ws02InterviewQuestions.docx
 bc01ws02CoverLetter.docx

You will save your files as:

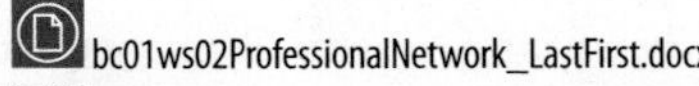 bc01ws02ProfessionalNetwork_LastFirst.docx
bc01ws02PlanResume_LastFirst.docx
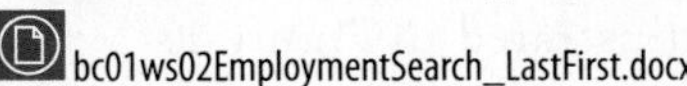 bc01ws02EmploymentSearch_LastFirst.docx
 bc01ws02InterviewQuestions_LastFirst.docx
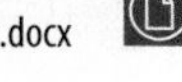
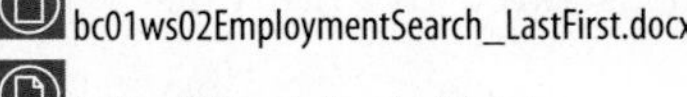 bc01ws02CoverLetter_LastFirst.docx

Exploring Your Career Options and Searching for a Job

The landscape of today's workplace is dramatically different from the past. As you begin exploring your career options and embark on a job search, it is clear that the way you search and apply for a job has changed significantly over the years. Gone are the days when you found your job in the classified section of the newspaper, printed your resume and cover letter on nice paper, walked into the business in your best outfit, and filled out an application in person.

Technology has changed all of this. The Internet and social media have made job searching both more accessible and more challenging. Developing a digital portfolio, building a LinkedIn presence, and utilizing corporate websites to both develop your brand and seek employment are common and necessary. If you are uncomfortable with using these tools, you will need to adapt and embrace the changes in job seeking or you will not find employment.

One thing, however, has not changed in the search for a job; you still need to make a good first impression, and convince the company you will be an asset, in order to be considered.

Prepare for Your Job Search

As competition for jobs is tougher than ever before, searching for employment takes time, effort, and energy. The better prepared you are for your job search, the easier it will be. Having a good resume and cover letter is not enough.

Before embarking upon any type of employment search, you need to (1) identify your interests, goals, and qualifications, (2) brand yourself to create a professional image, (3) build and grow your network, and (4) analyze your online presence.

Identifying Your Interests, Goals, and Qualifications

In order to choose the right career for you, take an inventory of your interests, goals, and skills. There are many self-assessment tools available. Most schools and universities have career centers to help with career planning and assessments. Some common career assessment tools may be available to you through your career center such as the Myers-Briggs Type Indicator or the Strong Interest Inventory. Take advantage of any opportunities such as job skills seminars, career days, or one-on-one career counseling that your career center may offer.

The Internet has a lot of career planning and job resources available. Many sites offer free self-assessment tools to assist you. The United States Department of Labor—Bureau of Labor Statistics publishes the Occupational Outlook Handbook (http://www.bls.gov/ooh), which has extensive online resources for job outlooks and jobs in demand. This would be an excellent starting point to begin your job search. This site showcases what jobs are currently in need of being filled and may fit your skill set and interests.

Projecting a Professional Image

As you begin to market yourself for a job, you need to evaluate your assets and build upon them to showcase to potential employers. Personal branding is the way to market you. **Personal branding** involves developing your image, personal style, abilities, and other characteristics to differentiate yourself from others. View your personal brand as your trademark; protect it and carefully manage it. Personal branding works much like business branding, except the product you are marketing and advertising is you. You need to create a sense of "standing out from the crowd" as illustrated in Figure 1.

Figure 1 Stand out from the crowd

In order to create your brand you must first take a personal assessment of yourself. Think about individuals who would be in competition with you; what makes them stand out and how are they branding themselves? Ask yourself the following:

- What are my core values and beliefs?
- What am I passionate about?
- What do I want to be known for?
- What makes me unique?
- When someone thinks of me, what will they associate with me?
- What skills, education, and training make me stand out?

You will also need to assess your weaknesses and liabilities and how to overcome them to present a positive, professional image. Some branding experts have suggested that you go as far as doing a personal SWOT analysis of yourself as you begin building your brand. **SWOT** stands for strengths, weaknesses, opportunities, and threats. Conducting this analysis can help discover your talents and opportunities as you pursue your career options. Figure 2 is a look at how to use the SWOT analysis in building your personal brand.

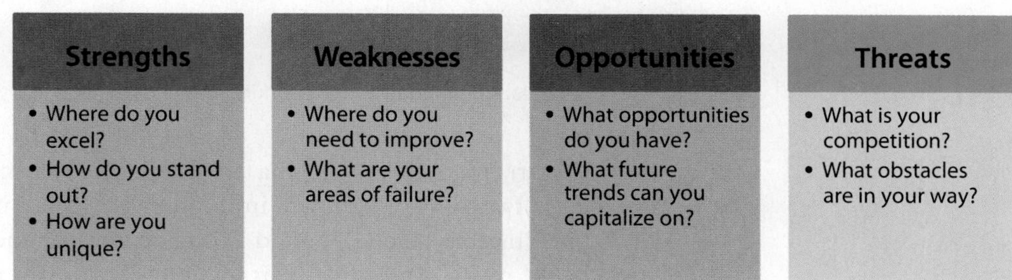

Figure 2 SWOT analysis—Build your brand

While developing your personal brand, it is important that you are completely authentic and honest. Do not portray yourself as somebody you think you should be, and do not pretend to be an expert in an area that you are not. People prefer honesty over exaggeration.

After you have taken the time to answer some of the questions posed, your next step is to begin to formulate a plan to brand yourself. The next two sections talk about two key ingredients to assist you with building your brand: networking and using social media tools.

REAL WORLD ADVICE | **Act As a Professional in the Workplace**

Dress and behave like the position you want, not the position you have. Professional behavior and attitudes often play an important role in who gets hired and promoted. You can start by taking note of your appearance. Appearance does matter and is remembered. Your attire should be professional and appropriate for the situation.

Building a Professional Network

It is all about networking. **Networking** is a process of making contacts with individuals who may be able to help you with your professional and personal goals. There is no one way to build your professional network. Networking builds relationships, and successful relationships take time. Seek opportunities to network and make real connections. Friends, family, coworkers, and other professionals you know can be a great starting point. Join professional organizations that are in line with your desired career goals. Do your research to find which organizations will be your best choices.

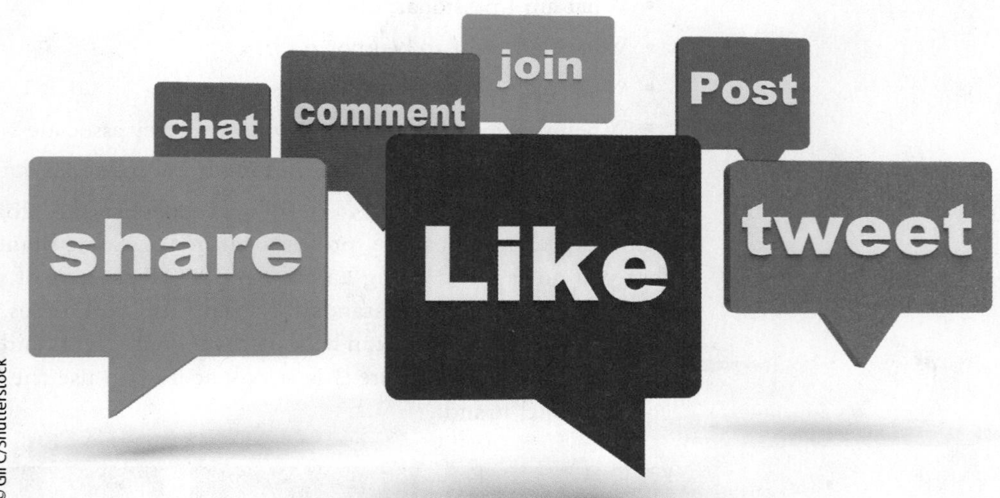

Figure 3 Social media tools for networking

There are many social media tools designed specifically for professional and personal networking as shown in Figure 3. Social networks such as Facebook, LinkedIn, Pinterest, Google+, and Twitter connect hundreds of thousands of people. These social media sites offer an array of opportunities to market you to prospective employers. This is a must in today's job marketplace. The key, however, is to make sure that your online profile is built carefully and presents a positive identity for you. You need to make sure that your online presence speaks directly to the audience you want it to. When someone leaves your Facebook, LinkedIn, or other social media site, what impression have you left?

MODULE 1

REAL WORLD ADVICE | Prepare Your Elevator Speech

As you begin to network, one of your challenges may be to "sell yourself" in a short amount of time. Appropriately named the "elevator speech," imagine yourself on the elevator with the CEO for your dream job. You have the time it takes to get from the bottom floor to the top floor to sell yourself. What would you say? Preparing this 20–30 second speech ahead of time can have several advantages, the most important being that you will be prepared for that important moment.

Take some time to analyze your professional network. Make a list of your most important contacts for a job search and then think about who they know that can help and expand your network. The following activity will help you to get started.

BC02.00 To Build a Professional Network

a. Start **Word**, click **Open Other Documents**, double-click **Computer**, navigate to the location of your student data files, click **bc01ws02ProfessionalNetwork**, and then click **Open**.

b. Click the **FILE** tab, and save the file in the location where you are saving your files with the name bc01ws02ProfessionalNetwork_LastFirst, using your last name and first name.

c. Look over the document. Fill in the information requested for three individuals who are part of your professional network that can help you in your career or job search. You will expand your network by providing the information for three individuals each of your primary contacts know.

d. Click the **REVIEW** tab, and then click **Spelling & Grammar** in the Proofing group. Correct any misspelled words and then proofread the document.

e. Save your document and exit Word.

Evaluating Your Online Persona—Would You Hire You?

Remember that everything you do online can be seen by others, including a potential employer. Use this to your advantage by making your online persona a positive one. Think of your online profile as a showcase of your talents and accomplishments. Make sure it is professional. Chances are a potential employer has "Googled" you before you even have a chance at an interview.

CONSIDER THIS | Have You "Googled" You?

What do you think you will find when you type your name into Google? Go to Google and find out. That is exactly what a potential employer may do. Employers are being cautious and thorough in their quest to hire the right person for the job. Did you find photos of you that would be damaging or hard to explain to a potential employer? Do you have unprofessional postings to blogs or other websites?

When you post to online sites, such as blogs, make sure your posts are well written and free of errors. What you "Like" on Facebook or "Follow" on Twitter can impact how others see you. These often tell a potential employer your views on politics, religion, interests, and hobbies.

As you begin to build your online persona, or clean yours up, consider these helpful hints to ensure a professional image:

- Never post photos that would make an unfavorable impression or cause you embarrassment.
- Do not criticize your present or past employer online.
- Be careful who you connect with online. Read their posts and make sure you are not connected with individuals who have negative, offensive, or unprofessional online information associated with them.

Research Employment Opportunities

Searching for employment can feel daunting and overwhelming. The timeframe of finding a job posting, submitting application materials, and being offered a position could take several months.

In previous sections, we discussed the importance of branding yourself and building a network to assist you when the time comes to look for job opportunities. Networking is listed as the number one resource for finding employment. Use your network to help you with leads to good jobs. The more people who know you are looking for a job, the better your chances of finding one. It is not only the people you know personally, but also the people they know. According to an article in the *Harvard Business Review,* almost 80% of job openings are never advertised; they are filled by individuals using their networks.

Use all of the resources available to you to learn about job leads. If you are just starting out in a career, most colleges and universities have career services that can assist you. Attend job fairs—these are excellent networking opportunities as shown in Figure 4. Join professional organizations where you may hear about potential job opportunities. Subscribe to blogs or job feeds.

Figure 4 Job fairs are excellent resources for potential openings

Online job boards are popular resources for potential leads. Table 1 lists examples of popular job boards available at the time this text was written. As online resources can change often, you will want to search for new and updated online resources that may be more relevant to your career choice.

Resource	Website
Monster	www.monster.com
CareerBuilder	www.careerbuilder.com
Craigslist	www.craigslist.org
SimplyHired	www.simplyhired.com
Indeed	www.indeed.com
SnagAJob	www.snagajob.com
LinkedIn	www.linkedin.com
TweetMyJobs	www.tweetmyjobs.com
Glassdoor	www.glassdoor.com

Table 1

Company websites are another great place to find job postings. Many companies only post career opportunities on their websites. Traditional methods such as classified ads in local newspapers still exist but are relatively small sources for job hunting.

Many social networking sites can also be a valuable resource for researching potential positions as well as being seen by potential employers. For example, LinkedIn has become the place for professionals to not only network, but also to look for jobs and be recruited by employers. For employers, there are several tools within LinkedIn that may be used for recruiting purposes, such as LinkedIn Recruiter, LinkedIn Job Postings, LinkedIn Employment Branding, and LinkedIn Talent Pipeline.

REAL WORLD ADVICE **Tap into the Hidden Job Market**

As many jobs are never advertised and are filled primarily through "word of mouth" or personal recommendations, it is important to know how to tap into what is often referred to as the "hidden job market." So how do you find out about these potential job opportunities?

- The most common way is through networking. Companies find it expensive to advertise a job so they rely on their networks and referrals to fill a job vacancy. Reach out to the individuals in your personal and professional network. Ask them to spread the word that you are looking for a job. Let them know that you are open to new possibilities.
- Try to connect with people within a company you are interested in working for to set up a phone or face-to-face meeting. Express your interest in finding employment in their company and why.
- Find a good employment firm or recruiter in your area of interest. These individuals often have inside leads to unadvertised positions.
- Post your resume to job boards. Many recruiters have access to these boards and use them to link up candidates to jobs.
- Get your profile on LinkedIn. This is one of the largest business networking sites. Many companies use this site to find potential candidates for positions.

If you have a company you are interested in with a job possibility, researching the business is crucial. Study the business and its products and services, read the most recent annual report, study its website to see which new products and services are being offered, if any, and identify its organizational practices. Think about the competitive landscape of the business.

Do not rely on one source, and never underestimate a potential career lead. The more places you look and the more strategies you use, the better your chances are of securing a position. Within the last few years, many businesses have begun offering virtual opportunities because of the continuing advances in and the increased use of Web 2.0 and social media tools. Web 2.0 technologies were developed to allow users to interact with other people on the web, rather than just click the links provided. Research shows there is a growing interest in virtual opportunities for full-time employment, part-time employment, and internships. According to the latest American Community Survey data, 3.3 million United States employees, not including the self-employed or unpaid volunteers, consider home their primary place of work.

The more you know about your chosen career field, specific job roles or functions, and types of industries, the more you are able to make a targeted search, as well as develop a list of potential businesses that are of interest to you. Your employment search may be influenced by specific types of industries such as non-profits, government agencies, or Fortune 500 companies.

You will conduct a search for potential jobs in your chosen field in the following exercise. Use a variety of methods as learned in this workshop to complete your research.

BC02.01 To Research Employment Opportunities

a. Start **Word**, click **Open Other Documents**, double-click **Computer**, navigate to the location of your student data files, click **bc01ws02EmploymentSearch**, and then click **Open**.

b. Click the **FILE** tab, and save the file in the location where you are saving your files with the name bc01ws02EmploymentSearch_LastFirst, using your last name and first name.

c. Fill in the information requested in the table by researching five employment opportunities in your chosen career field. Use a variety of sources such as the Internet, job boards, social media sites, college career and placement centers, or others of your choosing.

d. Click the **INSERT** tab, and then in the **Header & Footer** group, click **Footer**. In the drop-down list, click **Integral**. Replace the Author text with your name. On the HEADER & FOOTER TOOLS DESIGN tab, in the Close group, click Close Header and Footer.

e. Click the **REVIEW** tab, and then click **Spelling & Grammar** in the Proofing group. Correct any misspelled words and then proofread the document.

f. Save your document and close Word.

Create an Application Packet

As you apply for jobs, the screening process will determine whether you have an opportunity to interview for a job. If you do an average job of creating your application materials, you will be screened out. These materials need to be top notch in today's competitive workplace. The documents you submit tell a lot about you. Are you organized? Are you detail-oriented? Are you a professional?

Your application packet may include your cover letter, resume, career portfolio, and letters of recommendation. The following sections provide you with more information on each of these components.

Writing an Effective Cover Letter

Your cover letter may be the first impression a potential employer has of you. Make sure that it is professional and well crafted. It needs to pique the reader's interest so the reader takes the time to look over your resume. Hiring managers will filter out cover letters and resumes that have spelling errors or are poorly written. This is an opportunity to showcase your writing skills.

Even if a cover letter is not asked for, it is recommended that you always include one. A cover letter serves three purposes: (1) identifies the position you are seeking, (2) summarizes your qualifications and experiences related to the position, and (3) asks for consideration for an interview.

Review the job announcement and attempt to obtain a job description to tailor your cover letter and resume to the specific skill set for the job. This is an important step as it shows the potential employer that you have researched the company and know the needs of the company.

Your cover letter should be brief. It should be three or four paragraphs at the most and no more than one page. Figure 5 is an example of a cover letter.

Erica Thomas

222 Canyon Road ◆ Santa Fe, NM 87594 ◆ 505.555.1290 ◆ ethomas@centurytell.com

July 18, 2016

Ms. Lesa Martin
Painted Paradise Golf Resort and Spa
3356 Hemmingway Circle
Santa Fe, NM 87594

Dear Ms. Martin:

I was excited to see your job posting for a part-time virtual assistant at Painted Paradise Golf Resort and Spa in our career center at Paramount University. I am a highly motivated student, looking for hands-on experience as a virtual assistant, as I complete my final year of college. I am particularly interested in the hotel management field.

My education is focused on business management, but I have also completed advanced courses in Microsoft applications, including Word, Excel, Access, PowerPoint, and Outlook. I am familiar with using a SharePoint server to post web pages and content. For the past two years, I have been managing my web-based consulting firm that assists other college students in research and production of college documents, such as theses, reports, and resumes. I have clients from 15 states and 2 foreign countries. This experience has prepared me to work as a virtual assistant at Painted Paradise Golf Resort and Spa.

I have enclosed my resume. Additional qualification details are available at www.linkedin.com/pub/erica-thomas/24/46/634. I look forward to meeting with you to discuss my qualifications.

Sincerely,

Erica Thomas
Enclosure

Figure 5 Cover letter

As the purpose of the cover letter is to grab the reader's attention and persuade the reader to interview you, consider using the AIDA method discussed in Workshop 1 as you write your cover letter.

When addressing the cover letter, address the recipient by name whenever possible. If you are unsure, call the company and ask for the name and title. Often they will give the needed information. Make sure to ask for the correct spelling and gender. If you were unable to obtain a name, use Dear Human Resource Director or Dear Members of the Selection Committee. If you do find the name but cannot determine the gender of the individual, you may address the person using the full name instead of the last name. For example, Dear Pat Smith, for Pat Smith.

The first paragraph should grab the attention of the reader. This paragraph should entice the reader to want to continue reading. If you are applying for a position that was advertised, then you will want to include where you learned of the opening.

The next paragraph or two should build interest and desire. It should include your education, experience, and skills as they relate to the job. Make sure you clearly show the reader how your skills and qualifications can benefit the organization. Draw the reader to your resume without repeating what is in your resume. Be specific, and use as many examples as possible while staying within the confines of a one page format.

The final paragraph indicates a desire for an interview. Include contact information and the type of response you anticipate. Always detail how you will follow up.

A job may be obtained through solicited job openings. A **solicited letter** is written in response to a posting that a job opening exists. In some instances, however, you may write an unsolicited letter. An **unsolicited letter** is written to express an interest in working for a specific company even if a job opening has not been advertised. An unsolicited letter offers the advantage of having your letter and resume reviewed for a position that has not been advertised and provides you with the potential to expand your professional network.

In this exercise, you will prepare a cover letter for one of the positions you wish to apply for in your career field. The letter should be formatted in block style with mixed punctuation.

BC02.02 To Write an Effective Cover Letter

a. Start **Word**, click **Open Other Documents**, double-click **Computer**, navigate to the location of your student data files, click **bc01ws02CoverLetter**, and then click **Open**.

b. Click the **FILE** tab, and save the file in the location where you are saving your files with the name bc01ws02CoverLetter_LastFirst, using your last name and first name.

c. Replace the contact information at the top of the page with your information.

d. Using a job you found in the previous exercise, or another job of your choosing, select one to use as you write a cover letter.

e. Click below the contact information. If necessary, click **Show/Hide** in the Paragraph group on the HOME tab to display formatting marks.

f. Press Enter twice. Type the current date.

g. Press Enter twice and type an inside address.

h. Press Enter twice and type the salutation using mixed punctuation.

i. Press Enter twice and type the content of the cover letter.

j. Once you have completed the last paragraph, press Enter twice and add the appropriate closing and punctuation.

k. Press Enter four times. Type your name.

l. Click the **REVIEW** tab, and then click **Spelling & Grammar** in the Proofing group. Correct any misspelled words and then proofread the letter.

m. Save your letter and close Word.

Creating a Professional Resume

Your resume is an important marketing tool for showcasing your talent. A well-designed, error-free resume gives you the best chance of getting selected for an interview. Your resume and cover letter are often the first documents that a potential employer will look at to get an impression of you. A typical reviewer will spend between 30–60 seconds on their initial screening of a resume, so making yours stand out is the key.

A **resume** is a summary of your skills, accomplishments, and work history as it relates to a potential job. Determining what to include and what to omit can be difficult. Begin by making a list of your work experience, education, skills, awards, and accomplishments. Construct a basic resume that will become your starting place for each position you apply for. With the stiff competition for a job, it will be important that you write a targeted resume that is tailored for each position you are applying for.

Different industries can have different expected formats for your resume. Regardless of the type of resume, a basic resume will contain a summary of your personal information along with your qualifications, skills, education, and professional work experience, if any. Determining the format, layout, and design of your resume will be important in making an effective resume.

In the past, it was common to add an objective statement after the contact information. One of the newer approaches is to add a branding statement in place of an objective. Think of a **branding statement** as a type of sales pitch that sets you apart from others and tells the potential employer what you can do for them. It may include a description of you, your attributes, the value that you provide to your employer, and things that differentiate you from your competition.

REAL WORLD ADVICE | **Writing a Branding Statement**

As you begin to write your branding statement, consider the following:

- What are your skills?
- What are your passions?
- What three or four adjectives best describe the value you offer?
- What results have you achieved?

There are basically three types of resumes: chronological, functional, and blended or hybrid. Which type of resume style you choose will depend on your situation. Each type of resume has similar information, but how the content is arranged is different.

The **chronological resume**, as shown in Figure 6, identifies qualifications in order of occurrence, starting with the current or most recent position. It is the most often used and preferred by recruiters. This type of format shows how your career has progressed and is best used for jobseekers with a strong, solid work history. The downside of this type of format is that it will "flag" gaps in employment.

The **functional resume**, as shown in Figure 7, identifies qualifications by function without reference to the time of the performance or to a specific business and deemphasizes the where and when. This type of resume is best suited for individuals who are applying for jobs not directly related to previous work experience, or who have little work experience.

The **blended** or **hybrid resume**, as shown in Figure 8, is a combination of the chronological and functional. This format lists experience and education chronologically but also includes a qualifications summary section that allows you to highlight your qualifications pertinent to the position. This resume format is best used for individuals with extensive work experiences who want to showcase key skills that may be difficult to find in other formats.

LESA MARTIN

Event Coordinator ➤ Customer Care Specialist

Event Coordinator

Creative and results-driven events coordinator with 7+ years of experience in coordinating small and large events. Solid track record of meeting deadlines and balancing priorities producing superior results. Key skills include:

➤ Time Management ➤ Customer Care ➤ Project Management ➤ Teambuilding

Education

Certified Meeting Professional (CMP)
Bachelors of Science, Business Management, State University of New Mexico
Associate of Arts, Applied Business, Southern New Mexico Community College

Professional Experience

2007 – Present
Conference Event Coordinator, Painted Paradise Golf Resort and Spa, Santa Fe, New Mexico

Organize and conduct social and corporate events. Discuss clients' specific event planning needs. Plan the event venue, budget, and schedules. Negotiate space and catering needs. Maintain relationship with vendors. Coordinate events to ensure seamless execution. Establish new marketing and social media procedures. Design promotional materials and make changes as per clients' demands. Prepare presentations and secure sponsorships. Supervise a staff of 20.

2004 – 2007
Assistant Events Planner, Painted Paradise Golf Resort and Spa, Santa Fe, New Mexico

Interacted with clients to assist in planning events. Managed event budgets. Negotiated prices with vendors. Maintained liaison with caterers and managers. Worked with conference coordinator to synchronize events.

2002 – 2004
Customer Service Associate, Pro Shop, Painted Paradise Golf Resort and Spa, Santa Fe, New Mexico

Interacted with customers, providing excellent customer service. Answered customer questions, addressed customer issues, and communicated relevant information to the customer. Oversaw golf shop activities in the absence of the head professional. Managed the tee schedule.

1998 – 2002
Virtual Assistant, Self-employed while attending college.

Contacted potential clients. Produced documents as requested. Provided efficient and timely service.

8372 West Palace Avenue, Santa Fe, NM 87501 <> 505.555.2837 <> lmartin@centurylink.com

Figure 6 Example of a chronological resume

LESA MARTIN

Event Coordinator ➤ Customer Care Specialist

Event Coordinator

Creative and results-driven events coordinator with 7+ years of experience in coordinating small and large events. Solid track record of meeting deadlines and balancing priorities producing superior results.

Skills

- ➤ **Organizational and Project Management**: Ability to plan, prioritize, multi-task, lead, and manage concurrent tasks efficiently. Superior attention to detail.
- ➤ **Time Management:** Manage and plan schedules for clients, vendors, guests, and other groups involved in their event. Delegate tasks as needed for efficiency.
- ➤ **Communication:** Strong communication skills for dealing effectively with all internal and external customers, listen to and provide solutions for client needs. Able to remain calm under pressure.
- ➤ **Technical:** Proficient in Microsoft Office and web page design.
- ➤ **Creative:** Innovative and inspiring. Able to produce the "wow" factor for clients, and set our service level above the competition.
- ➤ **Negotiation and Problem-Solving:** Able to negotiate optimal solutions for clients and company, analyze problems, find and implement solutions quickly.
- ➤ **Team Member:** Excel at consensus building, collective approach; willing to roll up sleeves and pitch in as needed.
- ➤ **Financial:** Great at crunching numbers and staying within designated budget. Good at predicting unknown costs and contingency planning.
- ➤ **Supervisory**: Supervisor of a staff of 20. Oversee events from 25 to 500+ attendees.

Employment

Painted Paradise Golf Resort and Spa, Santa Fe, New Mexico 2002 – Present

Conference Event Coordinator (2007–present)

Assistant Events Planner (2004–2007)

Customer Service Associate (2002–2004)

Self-employed 1998 – 2002

Virtual Assistant

Education

Certified Meeting Professional (CMP)
Bachelors of Science, Business Management, State University of New Mexico
Associate of Arts, Applied Business, Southern New Mexico Community College

8372 West Palace Avenue, Santa Fe, NM 87501 ◀▶ 505.555.2837 ◀▶ lmartin@centurylink.com

Figure 7 Example of a functional resume

LESA MARTIN

Event Coordinator ➤ Customer Care Specialist

Summary of Qualifications – Event Coordinator

- ➤ Over 7 years of experience in providing event planning services to clients
- ➤ Well versed in creating, designing, and planning events
- ➤ Passion for creating unique experiences for clients
- ➤ Experienced in managing budgets and timelines
- ➤ Strong communication skills for dealing effectively with all types of personalities and situations
- ➤ Able to remain calm under pressure
- ➤ Excellent time management and problem-solving skills
- ➤ Proficiency in Microsoft Office and MS Project
- ➤ Supervisory experience, managing in-house staff of 20. Oversee events with 500+ attendees

Education

Certified Meeting Professional (CMP)
Bachelors of Science, Business Management, State University of New Mexico
Associate of Arts, Applied Business, Southern New Mexico Community College

Employment

Painted Paradise Golf Resort and Spa, Santa Fe, New Mexico

Conference Event Coordinator 2007 – Present

Organize and conduct social and corporate events. Discuss clients' specific event planning needs. Plan the event venue, budget, and schedules. Negotiate space and catering needs. Maintain relationship with vendors. Coordinate events to ensure seamless execution. Establish new marketing and social media procedures. Design promotional materials and make changes as per clients' demands. Prepare presentations and secure sponsorships. Supervise a staff of 20.

Assistant Events Planner 2004 – 2007

Interacted with clients to assist in planning events. Managed event budgets. Negotiated prices with vendors. Maintained liaison with caterers and managers. Worked with conference coordinator to synchronize events.

Customer Service Associate 2002 – 2004

Interacted with customers, providing excellent customer service. Answered customer questions, addressed customer issues, and communicated relevant information to the customer. Oversaw golf shop activities in the absence of the head professional. Managed the tee schedule.

Self-employed 1998 – 2002

Virtual Assistant

Contacted potential clients. Produced documents as requested. Provided efficient and timely service.

8372 West Palace Avenue, Santa Fe, NM 87501 <> 505.555.2837 <> lmartin@centurylink.com

Figure 8 Example of a blended or hybrid resume

Your resume should be written in active voice instead of passive voice. Active voice was discussed in Workshop 1. As you describe your qualifications and professional experience, use action verbs to grab your reader's attention. Action verbs give more impact and a stronger impression to potential employers. Look at the following two examples. Which one gives a clearer picture and has more impact?

Example 1: I was responsible for training employees on the new features of Office 2013.
Example 2: Developed and implemented a program to train 40+ employees on Office 2013.

MODULE 1

QUICK REFERENCE	Action Verbs for Your Resume		
Accomplished	Developed	Initiated	Optimized
Achieved	Exceeded	Led	Pioneered
Championed	Excelled	Leveraged	Produced
Collaborated	Executed	Managed	Recognized
Conducted	Formed	Masterminded	Re-engineered
Constructed	Formulated	Mentored	Spearheaded
Designed	Generated	Negotiated	Wrote

Writing an effective resume takes time. It will take several attempts before you have a resume that you will be happy with. Another consideration when writing your resume is the ongoing debate on the ideal length. Most industry experts suggest a one-page resume for entry level positions. If you are applying for a higher level position and have more work experience, a two-page resume is more common.

REAL WORLD ADVICE Use of Resume Templates

While resume templates are easy to use, consider whether or not the advantages outweigh the disadvantages for your specific needs.

Advantages	Disadvantages
Saves time and makes the process of designing a professional-looking resume much easier.	Has the potential of making you look lazy and unoriginal.
Helps provide structure by forcing you to determine what information is relevant to the position.	Limits the design options. Failure to portray your uniqueness. Too generic.
Assists with identifying keywords relevant to the specific position.	Does not always incorporate automatic spell check.

A growing number of businesses are using electronic scanning systems to digitally scan, store, and track resumes and cover letters. Some businesses will indicate if they scan resumes and provide formatting tips. Please look for these tips when you are researching information about the company.

A resume developed for scanning has a basic text format and no special formatting features, which changes the appearance of your resume, so you should consider developing two different sets of resumes, one for electronic scanning and one for printing.

Keywords are used during the scanning process. **Keywords** are nouns or short phrases that describe your experience, education, and other important information. These keywords are used to filter through large volumes of resumes that have been submitted electronically and stored in a database. Using technology, an employer will sift through theses resumes searching for the right mix of job-related keywords. To increase the chances of getting your resume accepted by electronic scanning systems, consider the following:

- Align the keywords listed on your resume with the required skills and qualifications listed in the job description.
- Use a 10-to 12-point sans serif font. Use capital letters only to add emphasis. Avoid the use of bullets, graphical elements, and other symbols. Key your name, complete address, and telephone numbers into the body of the resume and not as a header or footer. You want this important information to be read and not eliminated from the scanning process.

- Keep the layout simple. Keep all lines flush with the left margin instead of centering and indenting.

In this exercise, you will plan and gather information that you would include in a resume to send for a potential job you are interested in.

BC02.03 To Plan a Resume

a. Start **Word**, click **Open Other Documents**, double-click **Computer**, navigate to the location of your student data files, click **bc01ws02PlanResume**, and then click **Open**.

b. Click the **FILE** tab, and save the file in the location where you are saving your files with the name bc01ws02PlanResume_LastFirst, using your last name and first name.

c. In the **Branding Statement** or **Summary of Qualifications** section, type the relevant information for the job you are applying for.

d. In the **Education** section, add the relevant information. You should include the name and location of schools, dates of attendance, field of study, and degrees earned.

e. In the **Professional Experience** section, list your most recent work experience in reverse chronological order. Include job title, employer, location, work performed, and dates. Use action verbs.

f. In the **Achievements** section, list your academic or career honors, awards received, or any other achievements that merit mentioning.

g. Click the **REVIEW** tab, and then click **Spelling & Grammar** in the Proofing group. Proofread and correct any errors.

h. Save your document and close Word.

Building a Career Portfolio

A **career portfolio** is an organized collection of your professional documents and other items that demonstrate your skills, abilities, qualifications, awards, achievements, and experience. Think of a career portfolio as a more in-depth resume. It is basically a marketing tool for selling you. Some potential employers will require or ask you for a career portfolio, so you would be wise to have one on hand, as shown in Figure 9.

© oknoart/Shutterstock

Figure 9 A career portfolio is a record of your professional accomplishments

A career portfolio includes such items as your resume, references, awards, samples of your work, and letters of recommendation. As you begin putting together your portfolio, make sure it does not contain work from your current or past employer that would be considered confidential. Make sure to also remove any confidential information and names from all work showcased.

In today's digital work, some types of jobs call for electronic portfolios, but a traditional paper portfolio is still more common. If you are organizing a paper portfolio, organize your portfolio in a binder that you can bring along to interviews to share with potential employers. Table 2 gives some examples to include in your career portfolio, dependent of course, on the type of job you are applying for.

Work Experience or Credentials
Resume
Licenses
Letters of Recommendation
List of References
Education, Degrees, Certifications, or Awards
Diploma/Degree
Transcripts
Certificates
Samples of Work
Writing Samples
Software-Generated Documents
Evidence of specific skills—Public speaking, Leadership

Table 2

Compiling References and Letters of Recommendation

Begin to build a professional list of references that you can use for your job search. References should not be included in your resume. References should be on a separate page and would be sent along with the resume if asked to do so.

Before you compile a list of references, make sure you have asked for permission to use each individual as a reference. Your references need to be able to provide a positive recommendation. Using individuals who may give you a less than 100% positive recommendation will do more harm than good on your job search.

Typically, you will include a list of three references. They can include past or present supervisors or employers, coworkers, faculty members, or someone from a volunteer position. They should never include friends or family unless asked for. Friends and family members are usually considered good character references, not professional references. Keep your reference list up-to-date. If you have not maintained contact with one of your references for a considerable period of time, this reference should be replaced with a more current one.

Understand the Importance of the Interview

During an employment interview, you have an opportunity to highlight your work experience, skills, education, qualifications, and other personal qualities. The interview, as shown in Figure 10, enables the company to see if you are a good match and if you will fit into its company culture. This is also the time for you to determine whether this company is a good fit for you. It really goes both ways. Both parties get an opportunity to evaluate each other.

© Kzenon/Shutterstock

Figure 10 The job interview

REAL WORLD ADVICE | **Making a First Impression**

You only have one opportunity to make a good first impression. People tend to form opinions about others within the first 30 seconds of meeting them.

Most interviews consist of several types of interview questions. These will be contingent upon the type of position for which you are applying. Interview questions are typically a combination of icebreakers, general questions, and behavioral or situational questions. There are many career planning sites on the Internet that have a large reservoir of questions you can use for practice purposes as you begin to prepare for interviews. Here is a short list of common interview questions:

- Tell me about yourself.
- What led you to choose your major or field of study?
- Where do you see yourself five years from now?
- Was there an occasion when you disagreed with a supervisor's decision or company policy? Describe how you handled the situation.
- Describe a situation in which you worked as part of a team. What role did you take on? What went well and what did not?
- Describe a situation in which you had to work with a difficult person (another student, coworker, customer, supervisor, etc.). How did you handle the situation? Is there anything you would have done differently?
- How would a former supervisor describe you?
- Why did you decide to seek a position with our organization?

Every interview is different. The type of interview you will experience will vary according to the people conducting the interview, the company, and the type of job. You may be interviewed by one person or a panel, by phone or face-to-face. One interview may be required or you may have to return for a second round of interviews with a different group of individuals. Regardless of the type of interview, a successful interview requires thorough preparation. Here are some guidelines to follow when preparing for an interview:

- Conduct research on the company and the position for which you are interviewing. Learn as much as possible about the company. Review the company's website. If it has social media sites, check these out as well.
- Analyze the job by going back over the job description or any other information you have been able to obtain about the job. Try to determine exactly what skills and experience the company is seeking in a candidate and determine how you will showcase yours in the interview.
- Get your interview wardrobe together. Do not wait unit the morning of the interview to determine what you will be wearing. Remember that appearance does matter and, as discussed earlier, you only get one chance to give a good first impression.
- Practice responses to interview questions. Listed earlier are some typical interview questions. The Internet and the career center at your college or university may also have a list of interview questions you can use for practice.
- Gather any materials you will need during the interview. If you have been asked to provide a career portfolio, assemble it, making sure you have included all relevant materials.
- Ask how many people will be present at the interview and if you will need to bring materials for each of them.
- If you are unsure of the location of the interview, make sure to have the correct address and, if possible, take a trip to the location prior to the day of your interview so you know how long it will take you to arrive. You do not want to be late for an interview.
- Prepare a list of questions you wish to have answered at the interview. Remember, this is your opportunity to get a feel for the company you are interviewing for.

REAL WORLD ADVICE **Practice Makes Perfect**

As you prepare for an interview, take the time to practice your answers to interview questions in the mirror. Anticipate which types of questions may be the most difficult and prepare an answer. For example, if you were recently let go from a position, expect the interviewer to ask why. You need to be prepared for this question and comfortable with your answer.

On the day of the interview, arrive early. If you need to fill out any paperwork prior to the interview, allow yourself plenty of time. Make sure you have all materials needed for the interview, such as extra copies of your resume, cover letter, letters of recommendation, and a list of references. Turn off your cell phone before you enter the building.

During the interview, your verbal and nonverbal communication skills will be evaluated as well as your credentials. Here are a few pointers for making your interview successful:

- Start with a firm handshake with the interviewer. Do not address the interviewer by first name unless asked to.
- Watch your body language and choose your words carefully.
- Be totally engaged in the interview. Listening is just as important as talking.
- Smile and maintain eye contact.
- Take the time to respond to the questions asked, but avoid long and rambling responses.

- After the interview, ask what the next step is. When will a decision be made?
- Thank the interviewer and shake his or her hand.

After the interview, follow up with a thank you letter reiterating your interest in the job. Send your thank you letter within 24 hours of an interview. You can use this opportunity to express your interest in working for the company.

In the following exercise, you will write out responses to typical interview questions to better prepare you for a real interview.

BC02.04 To Practice Responses to Interview Questions

a. Start **Word**, click **Open Other Documents**, double-click **Computer**, navigate to the location of your student data files, click **bc01ws02InterviewQuestions**, and then click **Open**.

b. Click the **FILE** tab, and save the file in the location where you are saving your files with the name bc01ws02InterviewQuestions_LastFirst, using your last name and first name.

c. Add your first and last name. Include today's date.

d. Type your answers to each of the six interview questions posed. These questions are typical interview questions you may expect when interviewing. By practicing your response, you will be better prepared when you have the opportunity to interview for a job.

e. For questions 7 and 8, think of two questions that you might anticipate for the type of job that you are interested in that have not been included. Add the questions and then your responses.

f. Click the **REVIEW** tab, and then click **Spelling & Grammar** in the **Proofing** group. Proofread and correct any errors.

g. Save your document and close Word.

Prepare Other Employment Documents

In addition to the application packet or career portfolio, there are other employment documents you may need to prepare as part of your career search. These include thank you letters, acceptance letters, letters of inquiry, letters declining an offer, and possibly a letter to resign from a current job.

Writing Thank You Letters

Within 24 hours of your interview, it is standard to send a thank you letter, whether you are interested in the job or not. If you are hoping for a job offer, your letter should include why you wish to be hired for the job as well as briefly restate your qualifications and how you are the right person for the job. It is also an opportunity to add anything of importance that you were unable to talk about or something you wish to expand upon from the interview.

In today's digital world, it is common to send a thank you letter via e-mail. If you have corresponded with the company via e-mail for setting up your interview, then sending an e-mail after the interview is considered appropriate. If a decision is going to be happening soon, you may also want to use e-mail to ensure that your thank you arrives prior to the hiring decision. If the company is more formal and traditional, you may want to send the thank you letter the traditional way through the United States Postal Service. Figure 11 shows an example of a thank you letter.

Dean L. Stewart

36923 Lampher Circle ◆ Santa Fe, NM 87594 ◆ (505) 555-1120 ◆ dlstewart@centurylink.com

March 25, 2016

Mr. John Martin
Jones Enterprise, Inc.
5402 Center Avenue
Santa Fe, NM 87592

Dear Mr. Martin:

Thank you for taking the time to meet with me yesterday to discuss the Customer Service Manager position. I am excited to be considered for the possibility to join the team.

My 10+ years of experience in customer service, coupled with my strong management and data analysis skills have prepared me to manage a team of dedicated professionals like your company employs. You indicated that you needed a team player who can build trust in your employees and clients. I believe I am the right candidate to accomplish this.

Again, thank you for considering me for this exciting opportunity. Per your request, I have enclosed a list of my professional references. Please feel free to contact me if you need additional information.

Sincerely,

Dean Stewart
Enclosure

Figure 11 Example of a thank you letter

Writing a Letter of Acceptance

Even if you accept a verbal offer, write an official letter accepting the offer, as shown in Figure 12. Use the direct approach in writing this letter as learned in Workshop 1. Address the letter to the person who has extended the offer. Even though you have been offered a position, you need to make sure the letter is professional and well written. Your letter should be brief and include the following:

- A thank you for the opportunity
- Acceptance of the position
- The accepted conditions such as salary and benefits
- Confirmation of the starting date

Dean L. Stewart
36923 Lampher Circle ◆ Santa Fe, NM 87594 ◆ (505) 555-1120 ◆ dlstewart@centurylink.com

March 25, 2016

Mr. John Martin
Jones Enterprise, Inc.
5402 Center Avenue
Santa Fe, NM 87592

Dear Mr. Martin:

I am excited to accept your job offer for the Customer Service Manager position. I look forward to being part of the team at Jones Enterprise, Inc.

Per our phone conversation, my starting salary will be $55,000. Health benefits will be available after my 90-day probation period.

I will report to your office on Monday, April 18, 2016, at 9 a.m. to begin my orientation. Again, thank you for this wonderful opportunity.

Sincerely,

Dean Stewart

Figure 12 Example of a letter of acceptance

Declining an Offer

Sometimes, you may feel that you are not a match for the position, or other circumstances will prevent you from accepting the offer. Politely decline the offer and express appreciation for being considered, as shown in Figure 13. An indirect approach as learned in Workshop 1 is a better approach for writing this type of letter. Remember, you always want to leave the door open for future employment opportunities. Follow the guidelines listed here for writing a letter of refusal:

- Use an indirect approach
- Keep the letter short, friendly, and sincere
- Explain the refusal in clear, positive words

Dean L. Stewart
36923 Lampher Circle ◆ Santa Fe, NM 87594 ◆ (505) 555-1120 ◆ dlstewart@centurylink.com

March 25, 2016

Mr. John Martin
Jones Enterprise, Inc.
5402 Center Avenue
Santa Fe, NM 87592

Dear Mr. Martin:

I was overwhelmed with your generous offer of employment for the position of Customer Service Manager. However, after much consideration, I have decided to take another position that will better fit my skills and career goals at this time.

Meeting with you and the rest of the management team at Jones Enterprise, Inc. was a pleasure. What I heard and saw was very impressive.

Again thank your for your time and consideration.

Sincerely,

Dean Stewart

Figure 13 Example of a letter declining an offer

Inquiring About the Status of a Position

If you have not heard anything about the status of a position you have applied for, you can send a letter of inquiry, as shown in Figure 14. Request the status of the position and provide a recap of your interest and qualifications. Express your appreciation for the consideration. Consider these things as you write your letter of inquiry:

- Did you confirm your interest in the company?
- Did you recap your qualifications?
- Did you keep your letter short, friendly, and sincere?

Dean L. Stewart

36923 Lampher Circle ◆ Santa Fe, NM 87594 ◆ (505) 555-1120 ◆ dlstewart@centurylink.com

March 25, 2016

Mr. John Martin
Jones Enterprise, Inc.
5402 Center Avenue
Santa Fe, NM 87592

Dear Mr. Martin:

Time is going by very quickly, and soon I must make a job decision. Before I consider all of my options, may I ask the status of my application for the accounts payable specialist position with your company?

I was interviewed four weeks ago. At that time, you indicated that I was one of the top candidates.

I would like to reiterate my interest in this position and I am hopeful that Jones Enterprises, Inc. is interested in having me join their team. I believe that this position is a great fit. It would be both challenging and rewarding.

I would very much appreciate hearing from you soon.

Sincerely,

Dean Stewart

Figure 14 Example of a status inquiry letter

Resigning from a Job

Circumstances change and you may have to write a letter of resignation. If possible, give the required notice time, which is typically two weeks. Often, companies require you to put your resignation in writing, even if you have given it verbally. If you must do so, briefly state your reason and acknowledge appreciation for the training and experience you have gained. The indirect approach is the best strategy for writing a letter of resignation. Be positive and leave the door open for future employment, as shown in Figure 15.

Dean L. Stewart
36923 Lampher Circle ◆ Santa Fe, NM 87594 ◆ (505) 555-1120 ◆ dlstewart@centurylink.com

March 25, 2016

Ms. Elizabeth Perdue
Production Goods, Inc.
5600 North Mayfair Road
Santa Fe, NM 87592

Dear Ms. Perdue:

Please accept this letter as official notification of my resignation, effective April 8, 2016. My employment at Production Goods, Inc. as a Customer Service Manager has been an enjoyable and enriching experience. In the six years that I have been employed here, I have grown as an employee and individual. I appreciate your personal guidance and your advice.

In order to make the transition a smooth one, I have put together a list of essential projects and due dates to help my successor. I am available to offer assistance and/or training to the new individual. I can assure you that I will continue to maintain my normal high level of commitment to the job up to the time in which I leave.

Again, thank you for the opportunity I was given at Production Goods, Inc. I wish you and the company success in the future.

Sincerely,

Dean Stewart

Figure 15 Example of a letter of resignation

Understand Pre-Employment Screening

If you are looking for employment, the chance of being asked to undergo some form of pre-employment screening is likely. Pre-employment screening is often referred to as a background check. Depending upon the type of business, and the job you will be performing, the company may be required by law to do a background check. It is common to have a background check performed for jobs in education, health care, law enforcement, and financial or banking organizations.

Pre-employment screening is used by employers during the hiring process or before they offer a potential employee a job offer in order to help them make the right hiring decision. It is used to check the validity of what the potential employee has written in their resume, discussed in an interview, or put on a job application. Due to the liability that a company has, it is looking to avoid hiring individuals who could be unethical, be dishonest, or cause it to be involved in negligent hiring lawsuits.

Types of screenings that companies may use could include a criminal background check, your employment history, education verification, driving record, credit history, reference checks, and a search of the Internet and social networking sites. You may also be asked to have medical tests or drug testing. If you are asked to have a medical exam or drug test, it must be expected of all job applicants for the same job, and the exam must be job-related.

Some companies conduct pre-employment screening themselves, and others may hire a third party to do the screening. Regardless, they must follow the laws on what information they obtain, require, and ask for. In order for a company to complete a background check, the company must comply with the Fair Credit Reporting Act (FCRA) regulations, as well as state and federal laws. A company cannot do a background check without written consent from the applicant.

If a credit report is completed as part of your employment background check, typically the three major credit reporting agencies—Experian, TransUnion, and Equifax—provide an employment report that includes information about your credit payment history and other credit habits. These reports are used by businesses to help determine your level of responsibility.

REAL WORLD ADVICE | **Check Your Credit Report**

As you are preparing to apply for jobs, it would wise of you to obtain a copy of your credit report. Each of the nationwide credit reporting agencies—Experian, TransUnion, and Equifax—is required to give you a free credit report. This will allow you to see what a potential employer will be viewing if it uses a credit report as part of its background check for potential employees.

If a company does not hire an individual due to information obtained from a background check, it is required to notify the individual and provide the name of the company that prepared the report. It must also give you the information for your right to dispute the credit report.

Concept Check

1. Explain the steps in preparing for a job search.
2. List some of the resources you can use to research employment opportunities.
3. Describe the three resume formats. Explain when you would use each format.
4. What are some of the guidelines for preparing for an interview?
5. What other types of employment documents might you need to prepare?
6. Why do companies conduct pre-employment screening? What are some types of pre-employment screenings used by companies?

Key Terms

Blended resume 51
Branding statement 51
Career portfolio 56
Chronological resume 51
Functional resume 51
Hybrid resume 51
Keywords 55
Networking 44
Personal branding 42
Resume 51
Solicited letter 50
SWOT 43
Unsolicited letter 50

Visual Summary

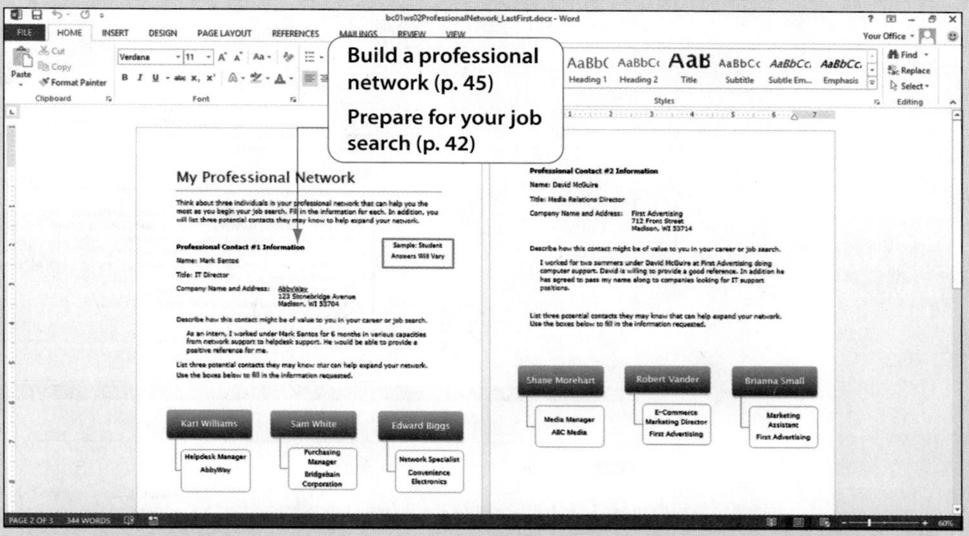

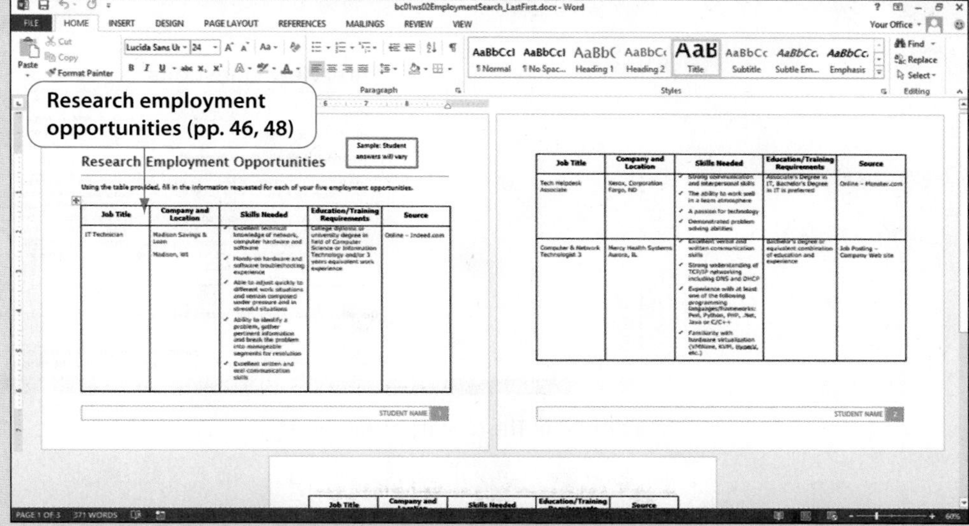

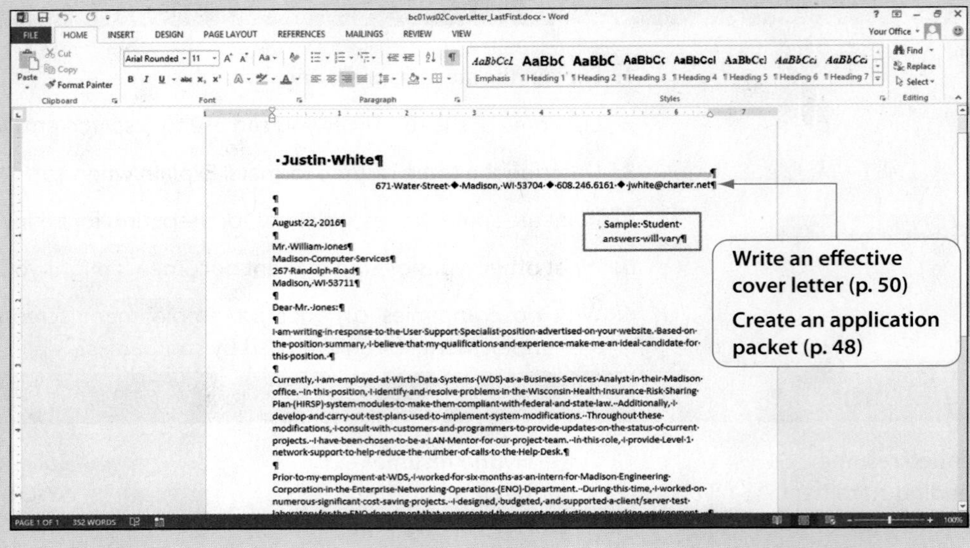

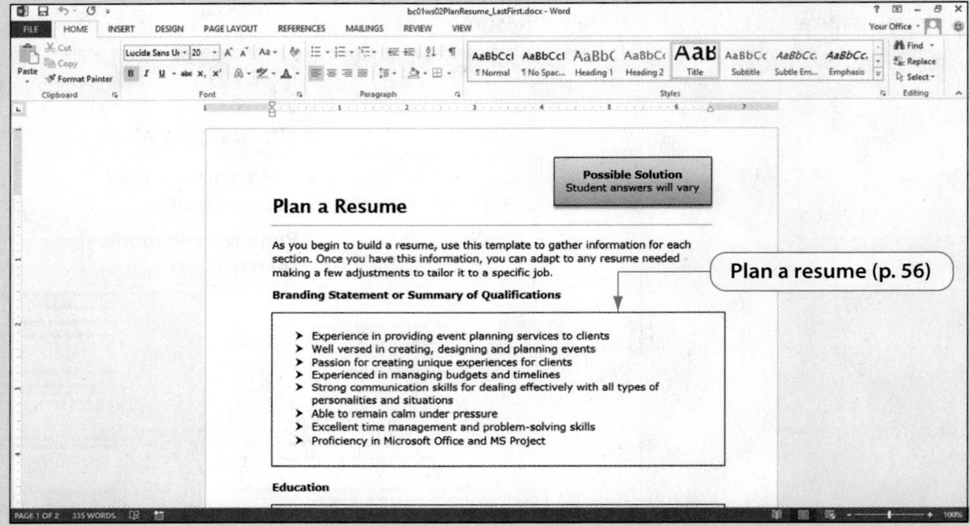

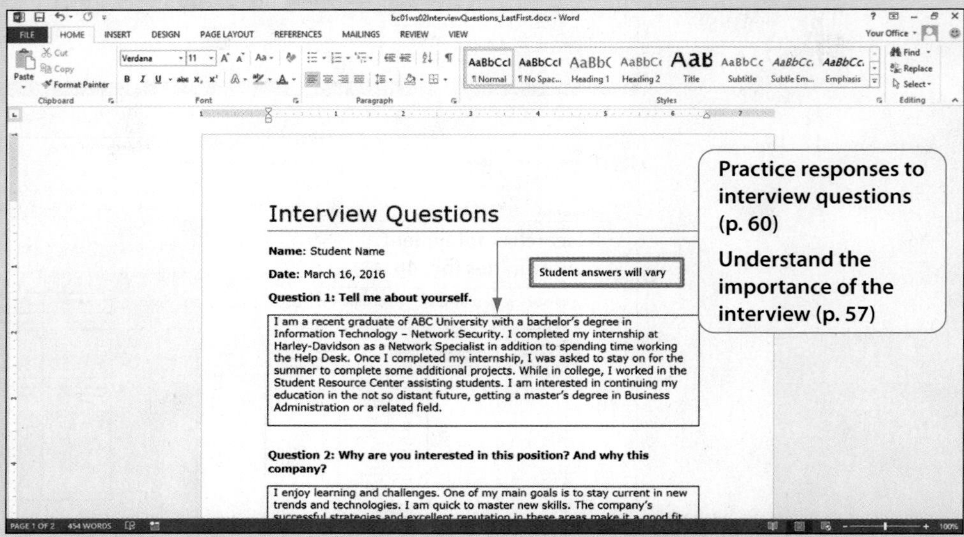

Figure 16 The digital portfolio final

Practice 1

Student data file needed:

bc01ws02ThankYouLetter.docx

You will save your file as:

bc01ws02ThankYouLetter_LastFirst.docx

Composing a Thank You Letter

It is always important to write a thank you letter after an interview. It reinforces to the interviewer your interest and can often make a difference in whether you are considered for a position. Assume you have just finished interviewing with Alex Haugom, of Castlemoor Enterprises. Write a thank you letter in block style with mixed punctuation thanking him for the interview. Add any needed details from a job listing that interests you.

a. Start **Word**, click **Open Other Documents**, double-click **Computer**, navigate to the location of your student data files, click **bc01ws02ThankYouLetter**, and then click **Open**.

b. Click the **FILE** tab, and save the file in the location where you are saving your files with the name bc01ws02ThankYouLetter_LastFirst, using your last name and first name.

c. Replace the information in the letterhead portion with your contact information.

d. Click below the letterhead. If necessary, click **Show/Hide** in the Paragraph group to display formatting marks.

e. Press Enter twice and type the current date.

f. Press Enter twice and type the following inside address:

   Mr. Alex Haugom
   Castlemoor Enterprises
   158 Second Street
   Santa Fe, NM 97794

g. Press Enter twice, and then type the salutation with appropriate punctuation.

h. Press Enter twice, and then compose an appropriate thank you message.

i. Once you have completed the last paragraph, press Enter twice and add the appropriate closing and punctuation.

j. Press Enter four times. Type your name.

k. Click the **REVIEW** tab, and then click **Spelling & Grammar**. Correct any misspelled words and then proofread the memo.

l. Once you have completed the letter, adjust the spacing of the letter so that it fits on one page. You may need to add some additional spacing between the letterhead and the date.

m. Save the letter and close Word.

Practice 2

Student data file needed:

bc01ws02AcceptanceLetter.docx

You will save your file as:

bc01ws02AcceptanceLetter_LastFirst.docx

Writing a Letter of Acceptance

You have just received a job offer from your dream company. You made a verbal commitment on the phone but need to follow up with a letter of acceptance. Write a letter of acceptance, adding your own information for the job. Include information on the title of the position, accepted conditions of salary and benefits, and your confirmed starting date.

a. Start **Word**, click **Open Other Documents**, double-click **Computer**, navigate to the location of your student data files, click **bc01ws02AcceptanceLetter**, and then click **Open**.

b. Click the **FILE** tab, and save the file in the location where you are saving your files with the name bc01ws02AcceptanceLetter_LastFirst, using your last name and first name.

c. Replace the information in the letterhead portion with your contact information.

d. Click below the letterhead. If necessary, click **Show/Hide** in the Paragraph group to display formatting marks.

e. Press Enter four times and type the current date.

f. Press Enter twice and type an inside address.

g. After the inside address, press Enter twice, and then type the salutation with open punctuation.

h. Press Enter twice, and then compose an appropriate acceptance letter for the position.

i. Once you have completed the last paragraph, press Enter twice and add the appropriate closing and punctuation.

j. Press Enter four times. Type your name.

k. Click the **REVIEW** tab, and then click **Spelling & Grammar**. Correct any misspelled words and then proofread the memo.

l. Once you have completed the letter, adjust the spacing of the letter so that it fits on one page. You may need to add some additional spacing between the letterhead and the date.

m. Save the letter and close Word.

Problem Solve 1

Student data file needed:

No data file needed

You will save your file as:

bc01ws02MDPCoverLetter_LastFirst.docx

Management Development Program Cover Letter

You have decided to apply for the Management Development Program at Painted Paradise Golf Resort and Spa. As part of the program, you will be exposed to the main operations and how each department works together; receive hands-on training in the areas of professional business etiquette, conflict resolution, and team building; and learn about various leadership principles and begin to understand and develop your own leadership style. Draft your solicited cover letter using block style with mixed punctuation.

a. Start **Word**, and open a **blank document**.

b. Save the document in the location where you are saving your files with the name bc01ws02MDPCoverLetter_LastFirst, using your last name and first name.

c. Create a letterhead for your cover letter. You would use the same letterhead when designing a resume. Make sure your letterhead includes all of your contact information.

d. Type the current date.

e. Type the inside address and salutation in block style with mixed punctuation using the following address:

Human Resource Director
Painted Paradise Golf Resort and Spa
3356 Hemmingway Circle
Santa Fe, NM 87594

f. Compose the cover letter. Complete the letter with the complimentary closing and your name using the correct letter format and punctuation. If you include an enclosure make sure to add the proper notation.

g. Proofread and correct any errors.

h. Save the letter and close Word.

Problem Solve 2

Student data file needed:

No data file needed

You will save your file as:

bc01ws02MDPResume_LastFirst.docx

Management Development Program Resume

Candidates for the Management Development Program at Painted Paradise Golf Resort and Spa must possess the following:

- Outstanding academic credentials
- Previous work experience
- Ability to work in a team environment and independently
- Demonstrated leadership skills
- Outstanding written and oral communication skills
- Demonstrated interpersonal skills
- Demonstrated advanced computer and analytical skills
- Experience in making presentations

You will create a resume that addresses the described Management Development Program requirements, as well as your unique skills, education, and experiences. You may select a chronological, functional, or blended or hybrid style of resume. Your resume must include a branding statement.

a. Start **Word**, and open a **blank document**.

b. Save the document in the location where you are saving your files with the name bc01ws02MDPResume_LastFirst, using your last name and first name.

c. Create a letterhead for your resume. You would use the same letterhead when designing a cover letter and other application materials. Make sure your letterhead includes all of your contact information.

d. Create your resume, using keywords from the described MDP requirements. Use appropriate layout and formatting.

e. Proofread and correct any errors.

f. Save your document and exit Word.

Perform 1: Perform in Your Life

Student data file needed:

bc01ws02OnlinePersona.docx

You will save your file as:

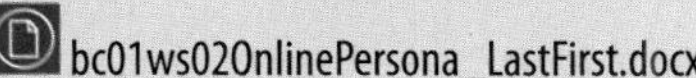
bc01ws02OnlinePersona_LastFirst.docx

Managing Your Online Persona

As you know, the use of online searches by potential employers is a reality. Whether we like it or not, the fact is that your online persona will likely be looked at and evaluated by a potential employer. The challenge is to develop and manage your online presence so that it portrays you in a positive and professional manner.

In order to assess what your online profile is saying about you, you will do some research on "You." In addition, you will begin to formulate a plan on how to use social media to enhance your online presence as you begin to "brand yourself" in a positive way online. You will use the worksheet provided to evaluate your online persona and formulate your plan.

a. Start **Word**, click **Open Other Documents**, double-click **Computer**, navigate to the location of your student data files, click **bc01ws02OnlinePersona**, and then click **Open**.

b. Click the **FILE** tab, and save the file in the location where you are saving your files with the name bc01ws02OnlinePersona_LastFirst, using your last name and first name.

c. Read the directions for completing the worksheet. Fill in the requested information. In Part 1, you will be researching and evaluating your current online presence. Part 2 will have you formulating your plan for creating a positive online image.

d. Proofread and correct any errors.

e. Save the document and exit Word.

MODULE CAPSTONE

As you prepare to enter the job market, one of the most important steps you can take now is to start preparing and assembling the documents you will need. In this capstone, you will begin to create and gather documents and/or other items to create a career portfolio. If you recall from Workshop 2, a career portfolio is an organized collection of your professional documents that demonstrates your skills, abilities, qualifications, awards, achievements, and experience. A career portfolio includes, but is not limited to, such items as your resume, cover letter, references, awards, samples of your work, and letters of recommendation.

Perform 1: Perform in Your Life

Student data file needed:

No data file needed.

You will save your file as:

bc01pf01Resume_LastFirst.docx

Creating a Resume

Create a resume using one of the three resume formats discussed in Workshop 2. The resume should be customized to a particular job posting that you wish to respond to. Even if you are not in the market for a job at this time, do some research on a potential job you may apply for and use this job posting to create your resume.

Your resume should be one page in length, unless you have substantial work experience and/or skills to fill a two-page resume. Use keywords or phrases common to the targeted industry to ensure you bring positive attention to your resume.

a. Start **Word**, and open a **blank document**.

b. Save the document in the location where you are saving your files with the name bc01pf01Resume_LastFirst, using your last name and first name.

c. Create a letterhead for your resume. Do not use a built-in resume template. You will use the same letterhead when writing a cover letter. Make sure your letterhead includes all of your contact information.

d. Create your resume using built-in Word headings and/or styles to ensure a consistent layout.

e. Proofread and correct any errors.

f. Save the document and close Word.

Perform 2: Perform in Your Life

Student data file needed:

No data file needed.

You will save your file as:

bc01pf01CoverLetter_LastFirst.docx

Writing a Cover Letter

Create a one-page cover letter to accompany your resume for the job posting used in the previous exercise. If you did not complete the previous exercise, find a job posting that you would be interested in responding to and write your cover letter.

a. Start **Word**, and open a **blank document**.

b. Save the document in the location where you are saving your files with the name bc01pf01CoverLetter_LastFirst, using your last name and first name.

c. Create a letterhead for your cover letter. Do not use a built-in cover letter template. If you have already created a resume, use the same letterhead for your cover letter. Make sure your letterhead includes all of your contact information.

d. Compose the cover letter using the block style format and mixed punctuation.

e. Proofread and correct any errors.

f. Save the document and close Word.

Perform 3: Perform in Your Life

Student data file needed:

No data file needed.

You will save your file as:

bc01pf01References_LastFirst.docx

Creating a List of References

Create a list of three professional references that you will include in your career portfolio or to accompany your resume upon request. Your references could be past employers, professors, or advisors who can verify your skills and qualifications and provide a positive and accurate description of you to the employer or company from which you are seeking employment.

Your list of references should match your resume and cover letter in terms of letterhead, font, and layout. It is not necessary for your list of references to be in alphabetical order. Your list of references could be in the order in which you wish them to be contacted.

a. Start **Word**, and open a **blank document**.

b. Save the document in the location where you are saving your files with the name bc01pf01References_LastFirst, using your last name and first name.

c. Start your list of references with your contact information. Use the letterhead format from your resume and cover letter to maintain continuity between all of these items.

d. Below the contact information, add the heading References. Select the heading and increase the font size to 20 pt., bold. You may wish to center the heading **References** on the page.

e. Below the heading, compose your list of three references. Use the format shown next, making sure the font size of the name is slightly larger and bold. Although it is not required to add "Mr." or "Ms." before a person's name on your list of references, it can be helpful if a person's gender is not obvious.

   Name

   Title/Position

   Department/Company

   Address

   Telephone number

   Brief statement as to how you know this person

f. Proofread and correct any errors.

g. Save the document and close Word.

Perform 4: Perform in Your Life

Student data file needed:

No data file needed.

You will save your file as:

bc01pf01RecommendationLetterRequest_LastFirst.docx

Requesting a Letter of Recommendation

As part of your portfolio, you will need to obtain two letters of recommendation. As a soon-to-be graduate, employers will expect you to get at least one letter of recommendation from a professor. It is highly recommended that you ask for a letter of recommendation face-to-face and not send an e-mail or leave a voicemail. However, at times, this may be necessary. To prepare you for requesting a letter of recommendation in writing, you will draft an e-mail that you could send to a professor to request that he or she write you this recommendation letter. You will use Microsoft Word to draft the e-mail.

a. Start **Word**, and open a **blank document**.

b. Save the document in the location where you are saving your files with the name bc01pf01RecommendationLetterRequest_LastFirst, using your last name and first name.

c. Compose the e-mail. In the e-mail, provide the professor with specific information to help him or her recall you and your accomplishments. Do not assume that the professor will agree to write a letter for you, so give the option to decline. Ask politely for a response to your request. Listed below are suggestions to include in your request:
   - When the letter of recommendation needs to be completed by
   - To whom the letter should be sent (name, title, and address)
   - The position you are applying for and details about the position (knowledge, skills, and experience needed)
   - List of the courses you have taken from this professor (course title[s], semester, year)
   - List of the kinds of work you may have done with this professor (thesis, portfolio, internship, independent study, etc.)
   - A copy of your resume and college transcript (unofficial is fine)

d. Proofread and correct any errors.

e. Save the document and close Word.

Perform 5: Perform in Your Life

Student data file needed:

No data file needed.

You will save your file as:

bc01pf01Sample1Reflection_LastFirst.docx
bc01pf01Sample2Reflection_LastFirst.docx
bc01pf01Sample3Reflection_LastFirst.docx

Assembling Work Samples

You will need to gather work samples to include in your portfolio that will demonstrate your skills, as well as the quality of your work. The samples selected are dependent upon the type of job you are seeking. Your work samples will need to be in hard copy as well as electronic format. Your samples may be copies of documents, spreadsheets, and/or presentations made from a computer software program. Pictures of projects are also acceptable if paper copies are not possible. Each sample should be error-free and represent the highest level of work you have achieved. If the example is from your place of employment, you will need to make sure it is not considered confidential and you have permission to use it in your portfolio.

For each sample you will include a reflection statement that describes why the example was created, as well as what skills and qualifications it represents.

a. Start **Word**, and open a **blank document**.

b. Using your first selected work sample, write a reflection statement for the sample. Be sure to include why this sample was chosen and the skills and qualifications it represents.

c. Save the document in the location where you are saving your files with the name bc01pf01Sample1Reflection_LastFirst, using your last name and first name.

d. Using your second and third selected work samples, again write reflection statements for these samples.

e. Save the documents in the location where you are saving your files with the names bc01pf01Sample2Reflection_LastFirst and bc01pf01Sample3Reflection_LastFirst, using your last name and first name.

f. Proofread and correct any errors.

g. Save the documents and close Word.

Perform 6: Perform in Your Life

Student data file needed:

No data file needed.

You will save your file as:

bc01pf01TitlePage_LastFirst.docx

bc01pf01TOC_LastFirst.docx

Finalizing Your Portfolio

You are now ready to assemble your portfolio and put together the final documents needed. You still need to create a title page and a table of contents. The title page will give your name and an appropriate title. You may want to include a relevant picture on the title page. Make sure, however, that you have the copyright permission for the photo you are adding.

a. Start **Word**, and open a **blank document**.

b. Create a title page, adding the appropriate title and your name. Be creative and add shapes, lines, etc., to add design to the title page.

c. Save the document in the location where you are saving your files with the name bc01pf01TitlePage_LastFirst, using your last name and first name.

d. Create a table of contents for your portfolio. List the items as they will appear in your portfolio. Include page numbers so that an individual can easily find items in your portfolio.

e. Save the document in the location where you are saving your files with the name bc01pf01TOC_LastFirst, using your last name and first name.

f. Proofread and correct any errors.

g. Save the documents and close Word.

h. Assemble your portfolio in a three-ring binder, following the instructions provided by your instructor.

Glossary

A

Abstract words Ideas or concepts.

Active listening Listening technique that involves listening with more than just your ears; it involves your entire body.

Active voice The subject is the doer of the action.

B

Barrier Anything that interferes with the sender's intended message reaching the receiver.

Biased language Language that stereotypes or unfairly categorizes an individual or group of people.

Blended resume A combination of the chronological and functional resumes. This format lists experience and education chronologically, but it also includes a summary of qualifications section to highlight qualifications pertinent to the position.

Block style Letter style in which the entire content is left-aligned and single-spaced.

Blog Website that has the look and feel of a journal.

Branding statement A personal statement used on a resume to differentiate an individual from their competition.

C

Career portfolio Organized collection of an individual's professional documents and other items that demonstrate their skills, abilities, qualifications, awards, achievements, and/or experience.

Channel Medium in which a message is sent to its intended audience.

Chronological resume Resume format in which work history is listed first, starting with the current or most recent position. Most widely used resume format.

Cloud computing Services offered on the Internet.

Communication The exchange of information from one individual or group to another.

Concrete words Explicit words that refer to definite persons, places, or things.

D

Digital communication The exchange of information between sender and receiver through a channel of transmission that is digital.

Direct approach Main idea is written followed by the explanation. Used for delivering good news or addressing unemotional issues.

E

Edit Checking for clarity and understanding.

F

Functional resume Resume format that focuses on your skills and experience, rather than on your chronological work history.

H

Hearing A physical ability that requires no additional intellectual effort if you are physically equipped to receive sounds.

Hybrid resume A combination of the chronological and functional resumes. This format lists experience and education chronologically, but it also includes a summary of qualifications section to highlight qualifications pertinent to the position.

I

Indirect approach A buffer explanation is written first. Used for delivering bad news.

K

Keywords Nouns or short phrases that describe your experience, education, and other important information.

L

Listening An active process that requires both hearing and thinking.

M

Memorandum Correspondence typically used to communicate information internally. Can be used for external communication.

Mixed punctuation The salutation is followed by a colon, and a comma follows the complimentary closing.

Modified block style Letter style in which the body of the letter is left-aligned and single-spaced. Date, closing, and signature block are left-aligned slightly to the right of center.

N

Networking The process of making contacts with individuals who may be able to help you with your professional and personal goals.

Nonverbal communication Communication that does not include words. Includes all unwritten and unspoken messages.

O

Open punctuation No punctuation is used after the salutation or the complimentary closing.

P

Passive voice Subject is being acted upon.

Personal branding Developing your image, personal style, abilities, and other characteristics to differentiate yourself from others.

Podcast Audio, video, or digital media that is distributed over the Internet to a computing device such as a personal computer or portable media player.

Proofread Checking for grammar, spelling, and punctuation errors.

R

Resume Summary of your skills, accomplishments, and history as it relates to a potential job.

Revise Checking to see if the document addresses its purpose and the required information is included.

S

Semi-block style Letter style in which the body of the letter is left-aligned and single-spaced. Date, closing, and signature block are left-aligned slightly to the right of center. Body paragraphs are indented 1/2".

Solicited letter Letter written in response to a posting that a job opening exists.

Stereotype Making assumptions that are not based on truth but rather on what is heard or believed to be true.

SWOT Acronym used to identify an individual's strengths, weaknesses, opportunities, and threats.

U

Unsolicited letter Letter written to express an interest in working for a specific company even if a job opening has not been advertised.

W

Web conferencing Interactive way to simulate face-to-face meetings between two or more participants at different locations using computer networks and software over the Internet.

Wiki Web page that uses online collaborative editing tools for building its content.

Index